THE COIN-TYPES OF IMPERIAL ROME

THE COIN-TYPES OF IMPERIAL ROME

By

F. GNECCHI
And
G. ELMER

ARES PUBLISHERS INC.
CHICAGO MCMLXXVIII

Exact Reprint of the Edition:
London 1908
ARES PUBLISHERS INC.
612 N. Michigan Avenue
Chicago, Illinois 60611
Printed in the United States of America
International Standard Book Number:
0-89005-225-5

PREFACE

There are many books about Roman coins, one should admit, and most of them prefer to deal with the Imperial period. Big 'Art books,' small and medium-sized 'illustrated handbooks,' Price-handbooks, Collection catalogues, multi-volume works aiming to form a 'Corpus,' pamphlets issued by coin-club groups and coin-dealers . . . So, the one who may ask the question, "Why one more book on Roman Imperial Coins?" positively deserves an answer.

There may be many, or too many books dealing with one subject; but this fact does not necessarily mean that the particular subject is completely covered. The special reason why many aspects of any subject may still remain not well covered, is that writers (and scholars sometimes) tend to concentrate their attention on the 'general view' or 'interesting details' approach, trying thus to make more attractive their own works. Since the coinage of the Roman Empire at first glance can be called a superb gallery including the portraits of all the Roman Emperors and many members of their families, it is natural that its most popular aspect will be connected with the art of those portraits and their place in the history of Roman art. Metrology, Inscriptions, reverse-types, mints and mint-marks, etc., will remain for the majority of the admirers of Roman Imperial Coinage at the level of information not always to be considered necessary or attractive. Let this information be left to be recorded in catalogues of museum collections and in scholarly journals. Collectors and art students are more numerous than epigraphists and economists and one who writes a book must always have in mind the ones who will buy this volume when it will be printed and distributed to the bookshops.

This is an exaplanation, I hope, of the reason that most of the books on the coinage of the Roman Empire pay more attention to the dramatic study of the portrait-obverses than the 'dull' and sometimes grotesque types of the obverses. For historians and archaeologists, however, those coin types and the inscriptions accompanying them can give information more valuable than the beautiful and artistic portraits. Questions like "Who was the divine protector of Marcus Vispanius Agrippa?", "Who was the emperor who used first Cybele on his coinage?", "When did the Greek and Roman gods cease to be used as reverse-types of Roman coinage?" . . . are more important for scholarship and research than the numismatic evidence on the size of Cleopatra's nose. And they become more valuable every day from the time that the history of the Roman Empire has started to use as primary sources the direct and indirect *testimonia* originating from the reverses of the coins.

The Coin Types of Imperial Rome, by F. Gnecchi, is a partial translation of his excellent handbook on Roman coins published in Milano by Hoepli. The value, however, of this partial translation lays on the fact that it was published as a help for the collectors and students of Roman Imperial coins, who were interested in knowing more from and about the reverse-types. The two 'Synoptical Tables' composed by Gnecchi as a brief survey of reverse types, and the alphabetically-classified texts about them, serve this purpose perfectly.

When this partial translation of Gnecchi's handbook was published in 1908, it appeared first in sections printed in the *Numismatic Circular.* Later, as the original used for reprinting testifies, all those sections were united in a book (printed in very few copies, as far as we can say from the few surviving copies of it), to which 28 plates were attached. The best that one can say about those plates (probably hurriedly made for the book), is that one can work better without them. As such they were omitted from this reprint edition.

To complete this unusual 'handbook' on the reverse-types of the Roman Imperial Coins, the student and the collector may express the wish that something similar existed on the obverse or portrait-types. Questions like, "What are the members of the family of Severus whose portraits appear on coins?", or, "Who was the last emperor who struck silver denarii?", or, "Do we have portraits on coins of all three of Nero's wives?", are not so easy to answer by using the conventional type of book on Roman Imperial Coins.

George Elmer's "The Portrait Coin-Types of Imperial Rome," a long list rich in details, answers those questions. Translated into English and added to Gnecchi's work, this list provides the information needed to complete it. There is no need to say much; scholars, students and collectors know how to recognize a useful source of information when they see one, the same way that they can recognize a book that can offer them nothing new from what they already have.

For a long time, during the years that I was preparing this volume, I thought that Cohen's amazing list of the reverse inscriptions of Roman Imperial Coins had to be added to it. This addition, however, would have raised the price at a level that many could call beyond their budget. The solution which I followed was very simple, and the best one available under the circumstances. A second volume, completely independent from the present one, will include Cohen's list, plus Egbert's and Cagnat's lists of the Latin Epigraphical Abbreviations, a work much needed for understanding the inscriptions on the obverses of Roman Imperial Coins.

Al.N. Oikonomides

THE COIN TYPES OF IMPERIAL ROME
F. GNECCHI

Preface 1
Gods, Demi-Gods and Heroes 4
List of Divinities adopted by each Ruler 6
Synoptic view of Gods, Demi-Gods and Heroes 8
I. The Divinities and their Relative Types 13
Apollo, 13. - Bacchus, 13. - Ceres, 13. - Cybele, 14. - Dioma, 14. - Dioscuri, 15. - Hercules, 15. - Aesculapius, 16. - Janus, 16. - Jupiter, 17. - Juno, 18. - Isis & Serapis, 18. - Mars, 19. - Mercurius, 19. - Minerva, 20. - Neptune, 20. - Roma, 21. - Romulus, 21. - Sol, 22. - Venus, 22. - Vesta, 22. - Vulcan, 23. - Other Gods, Semi-Gods, and Heroes, 23. - Pluto, 23. - Saturn, 23. - Prometheus, 24. - Earth (Tellus), 24. - Calliope, 24. - Oceanus, 24. - Anubis, Harpocrates, Apis, 24.
II. Allegorical Personifications 25
Recognition, 25. - Symbolism, 26. - Number, 26. - List of Personifications, 27. - Emperors who used Personifications on their coins, 27
Synoptic table of the Allegorical Personifications 32
Sketch of the Allegorical Personifications with their Relative Types and Symbols 36
Abundantia, 36. - Aequitas, 37. - Aeternitas, 37. - Annona, 39. - Bonus Eventus, 40. - Caritas, 40. - Claritas, 41. - Clementia, 41. - Concordia, 41. - Fecunditas, 42. - Felicitas, 43. - Fides, 43. - Fortuna, 44. - Genius, 44. - Hilaritas, 45. - Honos, 46. - Indulgentia, 46. - Iucunditas, 47. - Iustitia, 47. - Iuventas, 48. - Laetitia, 48. - Liberalitas, 49. - Libertas, 50. - Moneta, 51. - Munificentia, 52. - Nobilitas, 52. - Ops, 53. - Patientia, 53. - Pax, 53. - Perpetuitas, 55. - Pietas, 55. - Providentia, 56. - Pudicitia, 57. - Quies - Requies, 58. - Salus, 59. - Securitas, 60. - Spes, 60 - Tranquilitas, 61. - Uberitas, 62. - Victoria, 62. - Virtus, 63.
III. The Imperial Records 64
The Emperor, 65. - The Allocutions to the Army, 65. - The Congiaria, 66. - Departures or Arrivals or State Entries into Cities, 66. - Victories or Triumphs, 66. - Imperial Journeys through the

Provinces of the Empire, 67. - Happy Events in the Imperial Families, 67. - Other Representations of the Emperors, 68. - Memorial Coins, 68.
The Senate, 69. - The People, 70. - The Army, 70. - Provinces, Cities and Rivers, 71. - Public Events, 72. - Prayers for the Emperor, 73. - Games, 74. - Monuments, 74.

THE PORTRAIT COIN-TYPES OF IMPERIAL ROME
G. ELMER

Tables 5-20 00

THE COIN-TYPES OF IMPERIAL ROME

By

F. GNECCHI

THE COIN TYPES

OF IMPERIAL ROME

WITH 28 PLATES AND 2 SYNOPTICAL TABLES

BY

COMM. F. GNECCHI

TRANSLATED

BY

EMILY A. HANDS

Reprinted from the *Numismatic Circular*, 1908.

LONDON

SPINK & SON LTD

17 & 18 PICCADILLY, LONDON, W.

—

1908

THE

COIN TYPES OF IMPERIAL ROME

By Comm. Francesco Gnecchi.

PREFACE

The Imperial Roman Coinage, during the four centuries from the beginning of the Empire until the time of Romulus Augustulus, gives us, in uninterrupted succession, a series of little less than two hundred rulers.

In the obverse types of the coins we have a more extensive series of portraits than is generally known; in the reverse types a series so numerous and varied that it may almost be called infinite. While, however, the first has been repeatedly described and illustrated, the second, although numerous studies refer to it, has never been completely described.

Such will be the scope of this work in which I propose to give in synthetic form a general view of the coin types of the Empire.

The Roman Coinage, as is well known, is always the faithful reflection of the history, political, religious and social, of the Roman world, follows its vicissitudes of fortune regularly and constantly, noting and registering with its types not only the events but the evolutions of thought, thus becoming for us the most copious fount of information, a most authentic historical document.

A synthetic table of the coin-types is, therefore, not only a statistical curiosity — most interesting from the contrast between its exuberant riches and the extreme poverty of the present age in which we see the different nations striving to find a single type for their own coinage — it may also be the first step in successive inquiries, and to this initial study once accomplished, others will be able to give, in consequence, a much greater development.

The inquiry as to how and with what symbols every type was represented, the investigation into the origin and contemporary significance of each one, the observation as to what epoch, and why, and under which Emperor every type was introduced, in what period most widely used, when and by whom abandoned, or by whom resumed, the comparison between the original types and successive derivations, the evolution of the latter, the withdrawing of some type or of some detail fallen into disuse, these are all points of interest which, aided and illuminated by the coins themselves, may greatly add to our knowledge of the Roman world.

In the republican coinage the obverse was invariably consecrated to the divinity; so that for several centuries a sacred figure constitued the sign of the state coinage. When, with the advent of the Empire, the imperial effigy was substituted for that of the divinity on the obverse of the coinage, a very great number of types was represented on the reverse in which, however, the sacred element always predominated, so that the greater part of the money, say two-thirds, may be considered as dedicated to subjects either altogether sacred or at least connected with religion. On them are figured especially the gods of Olympus, demi-gods and heroes — those allegorical personifications which are one of the most singular and certainly the commonest characteristic of the Roman Coinage.

On the remaining third are included all those other types which refer to imperial acts, allocutions of the Emperor, congiarii, triumphs, arrivals, departures, journeys, and more rarely, to the senate and the people, to the cities and the provinces and also to monuments, temples, circuses, arches, bridges, gates &c. and an infinite number to public events.

It is evident that a strict division is impossible, and we meet with many types which may belong equally to two categories or which it is difficult to place in either; this however does not prevent the work from being divided roughly into three parts, devoting the first to gods, demi-gods and heroes; the second to allegorical personifications; and the third to imperial, civil and military types.

I certainly do not claim to offer a perfect work, but content myself with giving a sketch which may be altered, improved and completed in the future.

PART I.

GODS, DEMI-GODS AND HEROES.

The Roman Olympus is but a derivation from the Greek Olympus with modifications and additions of its own or taken from the neighbouring and allied races. The Roman instinct for assimilation, after having accepted as much as was adapted to its own genius, continued to develop gradually according to circumstances; and, as in the subjection of the world to the Romans, Rome increased little by little, and first the neighbouring tribes and then those more distant became Roman citizens forming one single family, so also in Olympus did the old Greek ideas of deity form one harmonious whole with the other local deities, Roman, Latin, Italian, European, Oriental or African, in accordance with the successive enlargements of the Empire.

The Roman Olympus consisted of twelve principal deities; in lower rank there follow many other divisions in regular hierarchical order which descend gradually to the heroes and to the legendary beings belonging either to heaven or earth. Of the twelve chief deities, ten, except for modifications of name and adaptations which we might call acclimatization, are taken from the Greek Olympus and are Jove, Juno, Minerva, Apollo, Diana, Mars, Vulcan, Mercury, Venus and Vesta.

Two more were added as national emblems, Janus and Quirinus. In secondary order follow other deities of heaven and earth, the sea, the winds and woods; the Sun, Moon and Stars, the Muses, the Graces, Cupid, Aesculapius, the Fates, the Dioscuri, Centaurs, Neptune, the Nymphs, Nemesis, Cybele, Terra, Ceres, Pomona, Saturn, Pluto, Proserpina, Hercules, Bacchus, the Satyrs, Silenus, Pan, Sylvanus, Faunus, Priapus and others.

But it is not suggested that these divinities maintain their hierarchical order on the coins and are represented on them in relation to their rank. Rome, for the special reasons to be explained hereafter, has the first place, and among the others there is a great diversity of treatment so that some of the deities are almost totally neglected, while to some other simple hero, Hercules, for instance, a splendid series of coins is dedicated. One fact worthy of notice is this, that while upon the coinage of the Empire, of Augustus and of Cæsar, masculine and feminine deities are represented without distinction, upon that of the Empresses only feminine deities appear, Apollo and Mars forming a slight and passing exception upon some of the coins and medallions of the younger Faustina.

In composing the catalogue of the divinities described with the relative types, and in drawing up a synoptical table of the princes who adopted them, I have chosen the most important numismatically, without regard to their Olympic rank; those especially which have a true sequence on the coinage and are commemorated by at least three Emperors, and I have contented myself with giving a short summary and *résumé* of those which make only a fugitive and incidental appearance.

It will be seen from the following tables, that, setting aside the goddess Roma as an exceptional case which we have explained, Jupiter was represented on their coins by 70 different rulers, Mars by 65, Sol 47, Venus 39, Hercules and Minerva 36, Vesta 34, Juno 31, Ceres 30, Apollo 28, Neptune 22, Diana 20, Aesculapius 13, Mercury 12, Cybele 10, Janus 8, Bacchus, Vulcan, Isis and Serapis 6, the Dioscuri 4 and Romulus 3.

THE FOLLOWING IS A LIST IN ORDER OF THE NUMBER OF THE DIVINITIES ADOPTED BY EACH RULER

Antoninus Pius	adopted	20
Hadrian	—	19
Gallienus	—	17
Claudius Gothicus	—	16
Caracalla	—	15
Commodus Septimus Severus	—	14
Marcus Aurelius Postumus	—	12
Trajan Lucius Verus Geta Aurelian	—	10
Vespasian Titus Faustina the Younger Tetricus the Elder	—	9
Augustus Valerianus the Elder	—	8
(The Roman Senate) Domitian Faustina the Elder Gordianus Pius Carausius	—	7

The following adopted six

Julius Caesar
Nero
Lucilla
Pescennius
Albinus
Julia Domna
Elagabalus
Philip the Elder
Æmilianus
Macrianus
Quietus
Victorinus
Probus
Numerianus

Diocletian
Maximianus Herculeus
Julian II

The following adopted five

Galba
Vitellius
Sabina
Alexander
Hostilianus
Trebonianus Gallus
Quintillus
Carus
Magna Urbica
Constantius Chlorus
Galerius
Maximianus
Severus II
Maximinus Daza
Maxentius
Licinius the Elder
Constantine Magnus

The following adopted four

Pompey Magnus
M. Antonius
Nerva
Volusianus
Salonina
Saloninus
Vaballathus
Tacitus
Florianus
Allectus
Constantine II

The following adopted three

Caligula
Claudius
Otho
Maesa
Mammæa
Philip II
Etruscilla
Cornelia Supera
Valerianus the Younger.
Crispus.

The following adopted only one : Brutus, Ælius, Soaemias, Orbiana, Otacilia, Regalianus, Severina, Magna Urbica, Alexander the tyrant, Licinius the younger, Fausta, Constantius I, Helena, Jovianus II, Sextus Pompey, Lepidus, Agrippa, Tiberius, Britannicus, Agrippina the younger, Domitia, Plotina, Pertinax, D. Julianus, Scantilla, Plautilla, Macrinus, Julia Paula, Aquilia, Maximinus I, Gordianus Africanus, father and son, Balbinus, Pupienus, Pacatianus, Trajanus Decius Herennius, Dryantilla, Decentius, Constantius Gallus, Valentinianus I, Valens, Valentinianus II, Theodosius I, Macrianus, Victor, Eugenius, Honorius, Placidia, Constantine III, Constans, Maximus, Jovinus (?), Sebastianus, Attalus, Jovianus, Valentinianus III, Avitus, Libius Severus, Anthemius, Euphemia, Julius Nepos and Romulus Augustulus.

The following placed no divinities on their coins : Cassius, D. Ahenobarbus, Q. Labienus, Fulvia, C. Antonius, Livia, C. Cæsar, Drusus, Nero Drusus, Antonia, Germanicus, Agrippina the elder, Clodius Macer, Domitilla, Marciana, Matidia, Didia Clara, Diadumenianus, Annia Faustina, Paulina, Maximus, Tranquillina, otapianus, Mariniana, Lælianus, Marius, Zenobia, Saturninus, Nigrinianus, D. Domitianus, Helena, Theodora, Romulus, Constantia, Delmatius, Hannibalianus, Vetranion, Procopius, Flaccilla, Constantius III, Licinia, Eudoxia, Grata Honoria, Petronius Maximus, Majorianus, Olybrius, Placidia and Glycerius.

SYNOPTIC VIEW OF GODS, DEMIGODS AND HEROES

	Apollo	Bacchus	Ceres	Cybele	Diana	Dioscuri	Hercules	Æsculapius	Janus	Jupiter	Juno	Isis & Serapis	Mars	Mercury	Minerva	Neptune	Roma	Romulus	Sol	Venus	Vesta	Vulcan	
Pompeius Magnus									●	●					●	●							4
J. Cæsar			●								●		●		●					●	●		6
C. Brutus	●															●							2
Cassius																							—
D. Ahenobarbus																							—
Q. Labienus																							—
S. Pompeius																●							I
Lepidus													●										I
M. Antonius									●	●			●						●				4
Fulvia																							—
C. Antonius																							—
Augustus	●		●		●					●			●			●			●	●			8
Livia																							—
Agrippa																●							I

	Apollo	Bacchus	Ceres	Cybele	Diana	Dioscuri	Hercules	Æsculapius	Janus	Jupiter	Juno	Isis & Serapis	Mars	Mercury	Minerva	Neptune	Roma	Romulus	Sol	Venus	Vesta	Vulcan	
C. Cæsar	·	·	·	·	·	·	·	·	·	·	·	·	·	·	·	·	·	·	·	·	·	·	—
Tiberius	·	·	·	·	·	·	·	·	·	·	·	·	·	·	·	·	●	·	·	·	·	·	1
Drusus	·	·	·	·	·	·	·	·	·	·	·	·	·	·	·	·	·	·	·	·	·	·	—
Nero Drusus	·	·	·	·	·	·	·	·	·	·	·	·	·	·	·	·	·	·	·	·	·	·	—
Antonia	·	·	·	·	·	·	·	·	·	·	·	·	·	·	·	·	·	·	·	·	·	·	—
Germanicus	·	·	·	·	·	·	·	·	·	·	·	·	·	·	·	·	·	·	·	·	·	·	—
Agrippina Senior	·	·	·	·	·	·	·	·	·	·	·	·	·	·	·	·	·	·	·	·	·	·	—
Caligula	·	·	·	·	·	·	·	·	·	·	·	·	●	·	·	●	·	·	·	·	●	·	3
Claudius	·	·	●	·	·	·	·	·	·	·	·	·	·	·	●	·	·	·	·	·	●	·	3
Britannicus	·	·	·	·	·	·	·	·	·	·	·	·	●	·	·	·	·	·	·	·	·	·	1
Agrippina Junior	·	·	●	·	·	·	·	·	·	·	·	·	·	·	·	·	·	·	·	·	·	·	1
Nero	●	·	●	·	·	·	·	·	●	●	·	·	·	·	·	·	●	·	·	·	●	·	6
Clodius Macer	·	·	·	·	·	·	·	·	·	·	·	·	·	·	·	·	·	·	·	·	·	·	—
Autonomous	·	·	·	·	·	·	●	·	·	●	·	·	●	·	·	·	●	·	·	●	●	●	7
Galba	·	·	●	·	·	·	·	●	·	·	·	·	●	·	·	·	●	·	·	·	●	·	5
Otho	·	·	●	·	·	·	·	·	·	●	·	·	·	·	·	·	·	·	·	·	●	·	3
Vitellius	·	·	●	·	·	·	·	·	·	●	·	·	●	·	·	·	●	·	·	·	●	·	5
Vespasianus	·	·	●	·	·	·	●	·	·	●	●	·	●	·	●	●	●	·	·	·	●	·	9
Domitilla	·	·	·	·	·	·	·	·	·	·	·	·	·	·	·	·	·	·	·	·	·	·	—
Titus	·	·	●	·	·	·	·	·	·	●	●	·	●	·	●	●	●	·	·	●	●	·	9
Julia	·	·	·	·	·	·	·	·	·	·	·	·	·	·	·	·	·	·	·	●	●	·	2
Domitianus	·	·	●	·	·	·	·	·	·	●	●	·	●	·	●	·	●	·	·	·	●	·	7
Domitia	·	·	●	·	·	·	·	·	·	·	·	·	·	·	·	·	·	·	·	·	·	·	1
Nerva	·	·	●	·	●	·	·	·	·	·	·	·	·	·	●	·	●	·	·	·	·	·	4
Trajan	·	·	●	·	●	·	●	·	·	●	●	·	●	●	●	·	●	·	·	·	●	·	10
Plotina	·	·	·	·	·	·	·	·	·	·	·	·	·	·	·	·	·	·	·	·	●	·	1
Marciana	·	·	·	·	·	·	·	·	·	·	·	·	·	·	·	·	·	·	·	·	·	·	—
Matidia	·	·	·	·	·	·	·	·	·	·	·	·	·	·	·	·	·	·	·	·	·	·	—
Hadrian	●	●	●	●	●	·	●	●	●	●	●	·	●	●	●	●	●	●	●	●	●	·	19
Sabina	·	·	●	●	·	·	·	·	·	·	●	·	·	·	·	·	·	·	·	●	●	·	5
Ælius	·	·	●	·	·	·	·	·	·	·	·	·	·	·	·	·	·	·	●	·	·	·	2
Antoninus Pius	●	●	●	●	●	●	●	●	·	●	●	·	●	●	●	●	●	●	●	●	●	●	20
Faustina Senior	·	·	●	●	●	·	·	·	·	·	●	·	●	·	·	·	·	·	·	●	●	·	7
M. Aurelius	●	·	·	·	·	●	●	●	·	●	·	·	●	●	●	●	●	·	·	●	●	·	12
Faustina Junior	●	·	●	●	●	·	·	·	·	·	●	●	●	·	●	·	·	·	·	●	●	·	9
Lucius Verus	·	·	·	·	·	·	●	●	·	●	●	·	●	·	●	·	●	·	·	●	●	·	10
Lucilla	·	·	●	●	●	·	·	·	·	·	●	·	·	·	·	·	·	·	·	●	●	·	6
Commodus	●	·	●	●	·	●	●	·	●	●	●	·	●	·	●	●	●	●	●	·	·	·	14
Crispina	·	·	●	·	●	·	·	·	·	·	●	·	·	·	·	·	●	·	·	●	●	·	6
Pertinax	·	·	·	·	·	·	·	·	●	·	·	·	·	·	·	·	·	·	·	·	·	·	1
Didius Julianus	·	·	·	·	·	·	·	·	·	·	●	·	·	·	·	·	·	·	·	·	·	·	1
M. Scantilla	·	·	·	·	·	·	·	·	·	·	●	·	·	·	·	·	·	·	·	·	·	·	1
Didia Clara	·	·	·	·	·	·	·	·	·	·	·	·	·	·	·	·	·	·	·	·	·	·	—
Pescennius Niger	●	·	●	·	·	·	·	·	·	●	·	·	●	·	●	·	●	·	·	·	·	·	6
Albinus	●	·	·	·	·	·	●	·	·	●	·	·	●	·	●	·	●	·	·	·	·	·	6
Sept. Severus	●	●	●	●	·	·	●	●	·	●	·	●	●	·	●	●	●	·	●	●	·	·	14
Julia Domna	·	·	●	●	●	·	·	·	·	·	●	·	·	·	·	·	·	·	·	●	●	·	6
Caracalla	●	●	●	●	●	·	●	●	·	●	·	·	●	·	●	●	●	·	●	●	●	·	15
Plautilla	·	·	·	·	·	·	·	·	·	·	·	·	·	·	·	·	·	·	·	●	·	·	1

	Apollo	Bacchus	Ceres	Cybele	Diana	Dioscuri	Hercules	Æsculapius	Janus	Jupiter	Juno	Isis & Serapis	Mars	Mercury	Minerva	Neptune	Roma	Romulus	Sol	Venus	Vesta	Vulcan	
Geta	●						●		●	●			●		●		●		●	●	●		10
Macrinus										●													1
Diadumenianus																							—
Elagabalus	●									●			●				●		●	●			6
Julia Paula																				●			1
Aquilia Severa																				●			1
Julia Soaemias																				●	●		2
Julia Maesa											●									●	●		3
Annia Faustina																							—
Sev. Alexander					●					●			●				●		●				5
Orbiana															●					●			2
Mammaea											●									●	●		3
Maximinus I																			●				1
Paulina																							—
Maximus																							—
Gordianus I																	●						1
Gordianus II																	●						1
Balbinus										●													1
Pupienus										●													1
Gordianus III	●						●			●			●				●		●	●			7
Tranquillina																							—
Philippus I	●									●			●		●		●		●				6
Otacilia											●						●						2
Philippus II										●							●		●				3
Pacatianus																	●						1
Jotapianus																							—
Trajanus Decius																	●						1
Etruscilla											●						●				●		3
Herennius													●										1
Hostillianus	●										●		●	●			●						5
Treb. Gallus	●									●	●		●				●						5
Volusianus	●										●		●				●						4
Æmilianus	●				●		●			●			●				●						6
Corn. Supera											●									●	●		3
Valerianus I	●				●					●			●				●		●	●	●		8
Mariniana																							—
Gallienus	●	●			●		●	●	●	●	●		●	●	●	●	●		●	●	●	●	17
Salonina											●						●			●	●		4
Saloninus										●			●						●			●	4
Valerianus II																			●	●		●	3
Macrianus	●				●					●			●				●		●				6
Quietus	●									●			●	●			●		●				6
Regalianus										●									●				2
Dryantilla											●												1
Postumus	●				●		●	●		●		●	●	●	●	●	●		●				12
Laelianus																							—
Victorinus					●		●			●			●				●		●				6
Marius																							—
Tetricus I	●						●	●		●			●		●	●	●		●				9

	Apollo	Bacchus	Ceres	Cybele	Diana	Dioscuri	Hercules	Æsculapius	Janus	Jupiter	Juno	Isis & Serapis	Mars	Mercury	Minerva	Neptune	Roma	Romulus	Sol	Venus	Vesta	Vulcan	
Tetricus II										●			●	●	●				●				5
Claudius Gothicus	●	●	●		●			●		●	●		●		●	●	●		●	●		●	16
Quintillus	●				●					●			●						●				5
Aurelianus	●							●		●			●	●	●	●	●		●	●			10
Severina											●									●			2
Vaballathus							●			●									●	●			4
Zenobia																							—
Tacitus							●			●			●				●						4
Florianus										●			●				●		●				4
Probus							●			●			●		●		●		●				6
Carus							●			●			●				●		●				5
Numerianus							●			●			●	●			●		●				6
Carinus							●			●			●	●					●				5
M. Urbica											●									●			2
Saturninus																							—
Nigrinianus																							—
Julianus II										●													1
Diocletianus							●			●			●		●		●		●				6
Maximianus Herc.							●			●			●		●		●		●				6
Carausius							●			●			●		●	●	●		●				7
Allectus										●			●		●				●				4
Dn. Domitianus																							—
Constantius Chlorus							●			●			●				●		●				5
Helena																							—
Theodora																							—
Gal. Maximianus							●			●			●		●				●				5
Gala. Valeria																				●			1
Severus II							●			●			●				●		●				5
Maximinus Daza							●			●			●				●		●				5
Maxentius						●	●			●			●				●						5
Romulus																							—
Alex. Severus										●							●						2
Licinius Senior							●			●			●				●		●				5
Constantia																							—
Licinius II										●							●						2
Valens tyr										●													1
Martinianus										●													1
Constantinus Magnus							●			●			●				●		●				5
Fausta															●					●			2
Crispus										●							●		●				3
Delmatius																							—
Hanniballianus																							—
Constantinus II										●			●				●		●				4
Constans I.													●				●						2
Constantius II.																	●						1
Nepotianus																	●						1
Vetranion																							—
Magnentius																	●						1

	Apollo	Bacchus	Ceres	Cybele	Diana	Dioscuri	Hercules	Æsculapius	Janus	Jupiter	Juno	Isis & Serapis	Mars	Mercury	Minerva	Neptune	Roma	Romulus	Sol	Venus	Vesta	Vulcan	
Decentius																	●						I
Constantius Gallus																	●						I
Julianus II	●		●							●		●				●	●						6
Helena			●									●											2
Jovianus												●					●						2
Valentinianus I																	●						I
Valens																	●						I
Procopius																							—
Gratianus																	●						I
Valentinianus II																	●						I
Theodosius																	●						I
Flaccilla																							I
Maximus																							—
Victor																	●						I
Eugenius																	●						I
Honorius																	●						I
Constantius III																	●						I
Placidia																							—
Constantinus III																	●						I
Constans																	●						I
Maximus tyrant																	●						I
Jovinus																	●						I
Sebastianus																	●						I
Attalus																	●						I
John																	●						I
Valentinianus III																	●						I
Eudo^a. Licinia																							—
Grata Honoria																							—
Petr. Maximus																							—
Avitus																	●						I
Majorianus																							—
Severus III																	●						I
Anthemius																	●						I
Euphemia																	●						I
Olybrius																							—
Placidia																							—
Glycerius																							—
Julius Nepos																	●						I
Romulus Aug^s.																	●						I
	28	6	30	10	20	4	36	13	8	70	31	6	65	12	36	22	96	3	47	39	34	6	

THE DIVINITIES AND THEIR RELATIVE TYPES

APOLLO

ACTIVS—AVGVSTVS— CONSERVATOR — MONETAE or MONETALIS—PALATINVS—PROPVGNATOR—SALVTARIS—SANCTVS.

The representation of Apollo passed on from the Republic to the Empire; it is not among those most commonly found, and, beginning with Augustus, it ended with Quintillus. Only two of the Empresses, the two Faustinas, adopted it. Apollo, whom the Greek mythology confounded with the Sun, calling him Phœbus, is generally represented nude and laureated but often wearing the long robe. His emblem is the lyre. He is sometimes found on medallions accompanied by other divinities.

BACCHUS

LIBERO CONSERVATORI — LIBERO PATRI.

It is strange that the god of wine and feasting, from the time of the Republic, upon the denarii of which the head only appeared, should have been introduced on the coinage with his licentious types by two Emperors who appear to have had fewer dionysiac proclivities than others. The great Hadrian and the good Antoninus Pius alone, on some of their medallions, made an exception to the traditional and constant propriety of the representations on the Roman coinage. The dionysiac feast on a medallion of Antoninus was reproduced on an aureus of Severus, in whose time Bacchus reappears with the title of LIBER PATER which he retained under Gallienus.

Bacchus is always represented as a youth and nude, crowned with ivy, with the thyrsus, the wine-cup or a bunch of grapes. On the first medallions he appears accompanied by Ariadne and some Bacchantes, upon those of Severus by Hercules. His favourite animal was the panther, which is represented alone as his symbol on a unique small bronze of Claudius Gothicus.

CERES

ÇERES — ÇERER — CERERI — CEREREM — CERERE — AVGVSTA — DEA SANCTA — EGETIA or SEGETIA — FRVGIFERA (or FRVGIS).

The fair and gracious goddess of the fields, the Queen of fruits, although she had not the honour of a throne in the highest assembly of the chief divinities, yet rivals Venus and Vesta in regard to the number of her representations on the imperial coinage. Her head, crowned with ears of corn, was already known on the consular coins; the whole matronly figure, wrapped in the peplum, with the emblems of the plough, ears of corn or cornucopia, as well as with the torch, as a reminiscence of her nocturnal wandering in search of her daughter Proserpina, carried off by Pluto, appears many times from Julius Cesar to Caracalla.

CYBELE

It is not until quite late that this African Goddess appears upon the coins and her representations are not very numerous. She was introduced by Hadrian and lasted only until the time of Caracalla, and the coins — medallions for the most part — upon which she figures, are always without inscription, or, at least, never bear her name; to which fact is owing the discussion, not yet ended, as to whether the goddess of the coins of Severus, Julia and Caracalla may be, not Cybele, but the tutelary goddess or Genius of Carthage who resembles her and has almost exactly her figure. Sometimes Cybele is seated on a throne between lions or drawn in a car to which are yoked four lions, as in the beautiful medallions of Hadrian and of Antoninus Pius; sometimes she is seated upon a lion or on a dog running.

Her symbols are the turreted crown, the sceptre and the tympanum.

DIANA

AVGVSTA — CONSERVATRIX — EPHESIA — FELIX — LVCIFERA — REDVX — VICTRIX.

Diana the huntress, the virgin of the woods, sister of Apollo, assumes various names; Diana or Artemisia on earth, Luna in heaven, Hecate in the infernal regions : on the imperial coinage she is generally represented as a terrestrial huntress, in a short robe, armed with bow and quiver, with one or two torches and frequently accompanied by a grey-hound or stag. The half-moon is her symbol when she is represented as a celestial goddess but occasionally on the imperial coinage Diana takes again the antique form of Lucifera in a swift biga, as she is often seen on the denarii of the Republic.

During the Empire her representations lasted from Augustus to Claudius Gothicus. The chief temple of Diana was in Ephesus, and her image, venerated in that temple, is reproduced on many cistophori, chiefly of the time of Hadrian.

THE DIOSCURI

Castor and Pollux, who had already figured on the coins of the Republic, were placed together for the first time under Antoninus Pius. Moreover one of the twins who is generally taken to be Castor, is reproduced on some medallions of Marcus Aurelius and Commodus, and then the Twins reunited appear upon a large series of coins under Maxentius.

They are always represented nude and the star shines over their heads; while, however, in the time of the Republic, we see them most frequently galloping on horseback, on the imperial coinage we find them constantly on earth with their horses held by the reins.

HERCULES

HERCVLI or ERCVLI

ADSERTOR — ARCADIVS — ARGIVVS — AVGVSTVS — COMES — COMMODIANVS — CONSERVATOR — CRETENSIS — DEBELLATOR — DEFENSOR — DEVSONIENSIS — ERINNANTINVS — GADITANVS — IMMORTALIS — INVICTVS — LYBICVS — MAGVSANVS — NEMAEVS — PISAEVS — ROMANVS — THRACIVS — VICTOR.

Though merely a legendary hero, Hercules represents one of the most important figures on the Roman coinage, contesting the field with Jupiter himself both by the enormous extent of his representations and the great number of appellations which accompany his name. Dedicated from the first to distinguish the Quadrans, and reproduced on various denarii of the Republic, his glorious series was continued during the Empire. Its first culminating period was reached in the reign of Commodus, who regarding him as his favourite and tutelary genius to the extent almost of identifying himself with him, caused himself to be represented frequently on the coins with his wives; then, after some time of comparative repose a second period was reached under Postumus, and a third under Maximianus Hercules which lasted until the time of Constantine. No other god, demi-god or hero is represented in so many ways or in such varied forms. The longest legend, which passed from Greece to Rome almost unmodified, is given in every detail on the Roman Imperial coinage. In the first period his types are the subject of a very great number of those marvellous monuments, the medallions of the most famous epoch, beginning under Hadrian and lasting to the reign of Septimius Severus, and upon which, together with the chief hero are found, gathered into the mythological legends, the other minor heroes and secondary figures such as Antaeus, Cacus, the Hesperides, Phosphorus, the Centaur, the Hydra, Omphale &c.

In the second period, under Postumus, Hercules is represented and described with all the appellations attributed to him by the fabulous legends.

In the third, under the four Emperors, Hercules is commonly associated, especially upon the medallions, with Jupiter and the Goddess Moneta.

Hercules is always nude; the club, bow and lion's skin are his ordinary attributes.

AESCULAPIUS

Aesculapius, the god of medicine, may be considered almost a duplicate of Salus; but he did not rival the latter in the importance of the representations on the Imperial coinage. Described for the first time by Galba, he next appeared on the medallions of Hadrian and Antoninus, then upon some coins of the family of Severus, and for the last time under Postumus and Aurelian.

Generally the austere figure of Aesculapius is represented in the toga with the staff round which is entwined the serpent. Rarely he is nude, and in that case it is perhaps not he but the African god of health who is represented.

JANUS

CONSERVATOR — PATER

Although there is much uncertainty of tradition as to the origin of Janus he may be considered as an eminently Roman deity. It is not known where he first appeared in Italy but he founded a city in Latium which was called Janiculum after him, and Saturn, who was expelled from heaven, was associated with his reign. His reign was peaceful, according to tradition, and Janus became known as the King of Peace. Such was the designation of his temple which was always shut in time of peace, as is recorded on the coins of Nero. The double head of Janus, looking to the East and to the West, the past and the future, was designed to represent the prudence of the two united races. *Jano Simulacrum duplicis frontis affectum est, quasi ad imaginem duorum populorum*[1]. And he had the honour of being chosen to represent the money type of ancient Rome, the As, while merely the semis was assigned to the mighty Jove. Such preëminence, which has an appearance of strangeness is

---

1. Servio ad *Aen.*, XII, 147.

explained in various ways; first that Janus may be considered as the god of beginnings; *ad eum dicuntur rerum initia pertinere*[1]. Thus Rome, renouncing Jove, of whom it was said *ab Jove initium*, assigned to him the first money as also the first month of the year. Moreover Janus was regarded as the symbol of covenants; *Janus faciendis fœderibus preest*[2], another reason for assigning to him the post of honour as representative of treaties and agreements. Finally it should also be taken into account that Janus was supremely a local deity, a thing to which Rome attached extreme importance.

But in spite of the fact that his type is imprinted upon the whole series of Republican asses in all its transformations, Janus left but a slight trace upon the Imperial coinage. After the time of the first triumvirate, which may be regarded as the transition between the Republic and the Empire, he appears only incidentally on some medallions or coins of Hadrian and Commodus, upon one denarius of Pertinax and upon one other of Gallienus.

Wherefore, if we have dwelt more fully upon his name than is proportionate to the importance of his appearance upon the Imperial coinage, it must be pardoned in consideration of his glorious past.

JUPITER.

IVPPITER, IOVIS, IOVI.

CONSERVATOR AVG, AVGG N.N., CAES, CAESS, CAESS N.N., ORBIS, N K, N K LYKC, P XV, LICINII AVG, PROBI AVG — CAPITOLINVS — CANTABRICVS (or CANTABRORVM) — CRESCENS — CVSTOS — DEFENSOR — SALVTIS AVG — DEVS — EXORIENS — EXVPERATOR — FORTIS — FVLGERATOR — GADITANVS — INVICTVS — IVVENIS — LIBERATOR — OLYMPIVS — OPTIMVS MAXIMVS — PATER — PRAE(SES or PRAEFECTVS ?) ORBIS — PROPAGATOR — PROPAGATOR ORBIS TERRARVM PROR PVGNATOR — SOSPITATOR — STATOR — TONANS — TVTATO— — VICTOR — VLTOR.

The Majestic head of Jove Optimus Maximus appeared in the first output of Roman bean-shaped coinage as the abiding symbol of the semis, and his figure and symbols hold a foremost place in the Imperial coinage; certainly the first, if we consider the multiplicity of his attributions, the different ways in which he is represented under one and the same Emperor, and the importance of the coins which represent him in every epoch. Jove is Conservator, Father and Custodian of the Emperor, and of Rome; Jove is the origin, the help, the hope, the propagator of the world; but he is also the terror of the world, the universal judge, the invincible, the

1. S. Augustine, *De Civitate Dei*, VII,7.
2. Servius ad *Aen.*, XII, 147.

vindicator. We must begin by giving an account of the numerous and varied representations, and indeed, we see him, a boy, astride the goat of Amalthea his nurse, in the island of Crete (Antoninus Pius, Saloninus), then seated majestically on his throne, the torso nude, the legs draped in the mantle, or nude, standing with the fulmen and sceptre, or with Victory and the eagle at his feet, which often bears the wreath in its beak; we see him as a colossal figure in the act of protecting the Emperor; we see him in his temple before which a scene of sacrifice is being enacted, or in a triumphal quadriga or a swift biga, in the act of hurling his thunderbolts against the giants.

Often, on the medallions of the good epoch, he stands between Juno and Minerva. The three figures are sometimes standing, sometimes seated; sometimes the three figures disappear and only their symbols remain to represent them, the eagle, the peacock and the owl (bronze of Hadrian and Antoninus Pius).

On medallions of the four joint Emperors he is often accompanied by Hercules and the goddess Moneta.

JUNO.

IVNO, IVNONI, IVNONEM.

AVGVSTA — CONSERVATRIX — LVCINA — MARTIALIS — REGINA — REDINA (probably in error for Regina). — SISPITA — VICTRIX.

The Superb Juno, sister and consort, often capricious and not always amiable, of Jove, is represented as a matron diademed and furnished with a sceptre, and having a peacock as emblem. Her statue in the temple is represented for the first time upon the coins of the Flavii, and her personification figures upon those of several Emperors and almost all of the Empresses up to those of Magnia Urbica.

Among the functions of Juno was that of presiding over the mint. On this account she sometimes assumed the name of Juno Moneta, and may thus be confounded with the goddess Moneta.

ISIS and SERAPIS.

ISIS FARIA — DEO SANCTO SERAPIDI (or SARAPIDI).

The two important Egyptian divinities made their momentary appearance only upon the small bronze coins which are attributed to Julianus II, Helena and Jovianus; but they are, perhaps, not all to be attributed precisely to that epoch. Isis makes a fugitive appearance also upon some medallions of Faustina the younger, and Serapis under Septimius and Postumus. Isis is always represented with the lotus flower on his head except for the few times that it is held in his hand. His emblems are the sistrum, a vase, a pail or a branch. Now he is represented seated to front in the act of suckling his son Horus; now standing semi-nude, upon the prow of a ship of which he holds the sail, then upon a car drawn by two mules or two hippopotami; now he is seated on a running dog or lion. When accompanied by Osiris, both terminate as sirens and hold between them a vase from which issues a serpent.

The head of Serapis is ornamented with the modius, he carries the sceptre and orb; but more often he is represented as a bearded bust.

MARS.

MARS, MARTI, MARTEM.

ADSERTOR — AVGVSTVS — COMES — CONSERVATOR — DEVS — INVICTVS — PACATOR — PACIFER — FVNDATOR PACIS — PATER — PATER PROPVGNATOR — PATER N K — PROPVGNATOR — VLTOR — VICTOR.

The god of war, the father of Romulus and Remus, makes his first appearance in his full Greek form upon the first bronze and silver Roman money coined in the Campagna, and then he is reproduced upon various denarii of the Republic. In the imperial series he contests with Jove and Hercules for the primacy from Augustus until the Constantinian era. Now nude, now in military array, he has sometimes a peaceful attitude but more often a warlike one. His emblems consist of an olive branch in the first case, and of arms and trophies in the second. A magnificent temple was erected in his honour by Augustus, under the title of MARTI VLTORI, a temple which is represented on the coinage of Augustus himself.

MERCURIUS.

MERCVRIO.

CONSERVATOR — FELIX — PACIFER.

Mercury, the heavenly messenger, the protector of artists, orators, travellers, merchants and thieves, is among those gods who figure least frequently upon the imperial coinage, although, of old, he was chosen to represent the sextans upon the bronze of the Republic. He was adopted, very rarely, by Trajan and the Antonines, and re-appeared only from the time of Gallienus to Tacitus.

He is generally represented nude, with the winged cap, and his symbols are the purse and the caduceus.

MINERVA.

MINERVA, MINERVAE
AVGVSTA — FAVTRIX — PACIFERA — SANCTA — VICTRIX.

Minerva, or rather, the warlike Pallas, for that is the character which this goddess commonly takes upon the Roman coinage, was chosen originally by the Republic as the symbol of the sestertius. Goddess of wisdom and of the arts and war, sprung full grown and armed from the head of Jupiter, Minerva is represented as a woman of masculine courage and strength in helmet and breast-plate, with a shield upon her breast and armed with lance and buckler. Minerva the warrior is represented in the act of defending herself with a shield or of hurling a dart, and in this character she is often placed upon the prow of a vessel; as peace-maker, with an olive-branch, as healer, in the attitude proper to Salus, feeding a serpent.

Her emblem is the owl. The type of Minerva was adopted immediately at the beginning of the empire, and her importance culminated under Domitian who chose her as the special protectress of the Imperial family.

More than 200 different coins of Domitian in every metal are dedicated to the warlike Pallas, and not only is her whole figure represented in various characters but also her bust, which we do not find on the coins of any other emperor.

Naturally Minerva is but rarely represented upon the coins of the Empresses, and but incidentally upon some medallions of the younger Faustina. Upon these, and upon other medallions of the good era she is often accompanied by Jupiter, Juno, Vulcan, or some other divinity.

NEPTUNE.

NEPTVNO
AVGVSTVS — COMES — REDVX.

Son of Saturn and Rhea, brother of Jupiter, the god of the sea appears on the first imperial coins of the two Pompeys, of Brutus, Augustus and Agrippa; and then at intervals until the time of Julianus II. He is always represented nude and bearded. The trident and the acrostolium are his attributes. Often his foot is placed upon a prow.

ROMA.

ROMA, ROMAE
AETERNA — AVGVSTA — BEATA — FELIX — HERCVLEA PERPETVA — RENASCENS — RESTITVTA — RESVRGENS — VICTRIX.

To complete its Olympus Rome placed among the principal deities its own founder, Romulus, with the name Quirinus; but we never find this name upon the coins and very rarely that of Romulus.

For these the goddess Roma was substituted. The importance given to her upon the Republican coinage, figuring as she did, from the beginning, upon the asses of Capua and upon the decussi of Rome, then upon the greatest number of the silver denarii, was the cause of her being preserved during the Empire; also, in any case, the figure of Roma was bound to come into common use if that of Quirinus was not adopted; Roma outdistanced Jupiter himself in the number of rulers who adopted her, amounting almost to a hundred; but it must not be forgotten that she owed this victory to the fact that by a slight change in signification she was able to prolong her life far beyond that of the pagans. When the new religion put an end to all the divinities of Olympus, and when Jupiter and Mars with all the other pagan deities, after the Constantines, and after a last rebound under Julianus II, were forced to disappear from the scene, giving up the field to the new Christ, Roma, changing in signification, came to be considered no longer as a goddess, but as a personification of the city and remained on the coinage permanently from the time of the Constantines until the fall of the Western Empire. This certainly would not have happened, if, instead of Roma, the god Quirinus had been placed on the coinage. But, taking the facts as here set forth, it would be almost impossible to trace a clear line of division between the goddess Roma and the Roma who was the personification or abstraction of the city.

Therefore the numerous coins having as type the wolf suckling the twins are attributed to Roma, whether as goddess, or as city; and this type which appeared first under Vespasian lasted with more or less frequency until the time of Constantine. To use the modern phrase, the very origin of Rome is here represented.

ROMULUS.

ROMVLO
AVGVSTVS — CONDITOR.

As has been said above, the name of the celebrated founder of Rome was eclipsed by that of Roma. He appears very rarely upon a few coins of Hadrian and of the Antonines, ROMVLO AVGVSTO, ROMVLO CONDITORI.

SOL.

SOL, SOLI

AVGVSTVS — COMES — CONSERVATOR — DEVS — DOMINVS IMPERII ROMANI — INVICTVS — PROPVGNATOR.

Sol is very little represented during the Republic and the early part of the empire; but he appears in a constant sequence from the time of Gallienus until Constantine II, and, indeed, until the most recent times in which we have representations of the pagan gods. Indeed, the series ends with Constantine II, and in it are represented also Jupiter, Mars and Sol.

Although almost always nude, Sol has occasionally the long robe and, as a distinction, the head radiate. He is always, when not in a biga or quadriga, standing, and bears, according to the occasion, globe or wand or the two things together.

Sometimes he is shewn in the act of crowning the Emperor.

VENUS.

VENVS, VENERI, VENEREM.

AVGVSTA — CAELESTIS — FELIX — GENITRIX (or GENETRIX) — VICTRIX.

Julius Cæsar always bore in mind his pretensions to a divine origin and represented Venus upon his coins, who, besides, had long appeared upon the Republican coinage. She was adopted also by many Emperors and by almost all the Empresses; but she ceased to appear with Gallienus and Saloninus. Nude, semi-nude or clothed, standing or seated, the goddess of beauty and love is represented diademed and with a sceptre and apple; sometimes she holds a dove and is often accompanied by Cupid or a dolphin.

VESTA.

VESTA, VESTAE

AETERNA — AVGVSTA — FELIX — MATER — MATER P R QVIRITIVM SANCTA.

Vesta, goddess of fire, follows almost the same course as Venus, beginning with Julius Cæsar and ending with Gallienus and Saloninus. The figure of the diademed matron by which she was represented bears the sceptre, the palladium, a torch or a simpulum (or more strictly a lamp); she is often represented in her temple, before which her priestesses, the Vestals, sacrificing, are sometimes seen.

VULCAN.

VOLKANO
DEVS — VLTOR.

The divine lame smith, the god of iron and fire, appears for the first time on the autonomous coinage of the Senate, then upon that of the time of Trajan and a few other Emperors until Claudius Gothicus, who dedicated a small bronze coin *Regi artis*.

He is represented with a short robe which does not reach below the knees, drawn to his side by a girdle, and with a pointed cap. His emblems are the hammer, pinchers and anvil.

On medallions of the Antonines he is represented in company with Jupiter by whom he stands preparing a fulmen, or with Venus, to whom he is giving a breast-plate for her lover Mars.

OTHER GODS, SEMI-GODS, AND HEROES.

Besides all the deities gathered into the one synoptic view with whom we are now especially occupied, there are many others who make a fugitive appearance, or of whom mention at least is made upon the Imperial coinage. Of these the Heavens, the Earth, the Infernal Regions and the Ocean contribute their legends and traditions.

Pluto, brother of Jupiter, who by the Romans, was counted not only among the twelve principal deities, but among the special eight whom, only, it was permitted to represent as statues in gold, silver, or ivory, has very little connection with numismatics. The moneyers appear to have preferred the gods of Heaven, Earth and the Sea to those of the Infernal Regions. We find Pluto only on a certain rare coin of Elagabalus, and he is represented seated, wrapped in an ample robe, with Cerberus at his feet.

Saturn, although the father of Jupiter, not only is not placed among the chief gods of Olympus, but is rather neglected, as if dethroned by his son and reduced to the condition of a mere mortal, and his memory is not recorded among the Romans except by the Saturnalia which were celebrated in memory of the age of gold over which he presided. Saturn was confused with Chronos by the Greeks, that is, with Time. The god who devoured his own sons is merely an allegory of Time who consumes all the years that pass. It is in this sense that we see Saturn, or Time, represented on a bronze of Trajan with the reaping hook, and upon a medallion of Commodus where he holds the circle of the year from which issue four children representing the four seasons. It is to Time that the bronze of Hadrian and Antoninus Pius refer which represent the Zodiac.

Prometheus. The unfortunate bringer of fire to man makes a single and fugitive appearance on a medallion of Antoninus Pius, on which he is represented in the act of forming a woman in the presence of Minerva. And with Prometheus we may also mention the *Argonauts*, the *Centaurs*, *Cacus*, *Telesphorus* and other legendary heroes.

The Earth (Tellus), symbol of fecundity, appears in the time of Hadrian. She is figured as a woman, sometimes standing with a plough or other agricultural implement or the cornucopiæ, sometimes seated leaning against a chest full of ears of corn and with her hand resting on a globe. On the medallions, the four children symbolizing the seasons form a crown above the globe.

Then follow the other terrestrial divinities; *Pomona* and *Flora*, *Pan*, *Sylvanus*, *Marsyas*, *Priapus*, the *Fauns*, the *Sileni*, the *Satyrs*, the *Centaurs*, the *Giants*, *Atalanta*, and the *God of Boundaries*, who all make their more or less fugitive appearance upon the numerous medallions of the Antonines, upon which the whole mythology is fully displayed. The Graces and Muses also are mentioned, but of the latter only *Calliope* has the honour of figuring with her name upon a rare bronze coin of Probus.

Oceanus is represented on the coins as are also some rivers, which, however, are to be considered rather as geographical expressions than as divinities, if we except the Nile which appeared in the time of Julianus the philosopher (DEO SANCTO NILO).

At this time also *Anubis*, *Harpocrates*, the bull *Apis*, and the *Sphinx* were imported from Egypt with Serapis and Isis Faria. But the Sphinx had made its first appearance, though perhaps not with the signification of divinity, upon a silver Asiatic medallion or upon an aureus of Augustus and of Trajan.

Lastly, among the divinities exceptionally represented or merely invoked we may note with a view to complete the long series, the gods of Augury (Septimus Severus DIS AVSPICIBVS), the gods of Marriage (Crispina DIS CONIVGALIBVS), the Custodian gods (Pertinax DIS CVSTODIBVS), the gods of Birth (Crispina DIS GENITALIBVS), the gods of Parentage (Pertinax DIS GENITORIBVS), the Family gods (Geta DI PATRII), the gods of Rearing (Saloninus DII NVTRITORES), and the Conquering Fates (Diocletian FATIS VICTRICIBVS).

PART II.

ALLEGORICAL PERSONIFICATIONS.

Allegorical personifications constituted a real characteristic of the Roman system of coinage. Rome the Assimilator, after having added the local deities and those of the imperial provinces to the Greek Olympus, created a great number of new deities which appeared suitable as fixing an abstract idea, or as personifying an allegory by means of which the people were educated and their minds more easily impressed. It was in this way that *Abundantia*, *Salus*, *Felicitas*, *Pax* were personified and deified, and also all the civil and military virtues, beautiful objects and various desires; and to these Personifications, as to real deities, statues were raised, temples and altars erected, and sacrifices consumed, not only in Rome but in all the cities of the Empire. By degrees they assumed a preponderating importance, if not as to rank, at least in numbers, so that in this respect they undoubtedly hold the first place in the coinage.

Each of these divinities is represented in one or more forms, and it is natural to suppose that the figures shewn to us by the coins are only reproductions of the statues erected to these divinities. But, if there remain only some isolated examples, it is to the very great number of coins remaining to us that we owe the perfect knowledge of that marvellous and rich series, which is not to be met with in any other system of coinage ancient or modern. The types of each one, once established, continue constant and unalterable, except for variations owing to the change in art, during the course of centuries; and the attributes proper to each, although at all times very numerous, are scrupulously observed. Begun in the very first years of the Empire, and some of them even in the time of the Republic, they lasted until the fall of the Western Empire, after which, the changed costumes and customs, the new religion which came as a complete surprise upon the Roman world, the decadence of art and other lesser events, caused them by degrees to be totally lost as numerous other types were lost, and to give place to the niggardly and rough Byzantine types, which betokened the artistic, moral and political decadence of the Empire.

The Personifications on the coins are almost always accompanied by the relative legend; sometimes, however, this is wanting or they substituted for it another, which, if it is not the indication of a date in continuation of the legend on the obverse, is one entirely unconnected with the subject.

Thus, for example, on many coins of Trajan we find several

Personifications, Pax, Victoria, Securitas, Salus, &c., invariably accompanied by the legend then in use on the money of that Emperor; SPQR OPTIMO PRINCIPI, and upon gold, silver and bronze money of many Emperors, the same coins bear only legends, as : COS III, or P M TR P COS II or III or IV, TR P IMP V, VI or VII, COS V P P and so on.

The Personifications, however, in spite of the want of the relative legend, are always easily recognized by their types, by their attitudes, clothing and symbols.

There is one case in which, without great practice, it is possible to make a mistake and it may be noted here once for all—it is when the legend relates to a Personification but does not correspond with the one represented on the coin. This never occurs in the best time of the Empire and is always exceptional in later times; but it happens rather frequently in barbarous times and in the more irregular mints. Especially under the tyrants it is not unusual to find, for example, the legend FORTVNA with the type of Salus, SALVS with the type of Victory, Pax, or other similar mistaken types. For these reasons the money of the Tyrants, and, especially, that of Carausius and the Tetrici, cannot be considered in the argument. They are to be treated simply as barbaric errors, and I take no notice of them, contenting myself with mentioning the fact.

*
* *

The Personification is not seldom replaced by a simple symbol. Thus an Antoninianus of Carus, with the legend ABVNDANTIA, represents a galley, and the allusion is sufficiently evident; on another Antoninianus of Tetricus, with the same legend, ABVNDANTIA, the instruments of sacrifice are represented, signifying, probably, a sacrifice offered in thanks to the divinity for having granted abundance. PIETAS is sometimes represented by a temple or the instruments of sacrifice; VICTORIA by a trophy and so on. Such examples are frequent at all times, nor are they difficult to interpret.

*
* *

From the beginning of the Empire until the fall of the Western Empire there are 170 names of Emperors, Cæsars, and Empresses who adopted allegorical Personifications on their coinage : there are forty of these counting only those which are true Personifications, although a true and precise limit cannot be assigned, and other representations have a clear right to make part of the series, as for example, *Disciplina, Beatitudo, Religio, Tutela, Utilitas, Humanitas,* and a few others which it is not easy to define as being true Personifications or simple abstractions.

But, setting aside all those which might be questioned I confine myself to the following list :

Abundantia	Liberalitas
Aequitas	Libertas
Aeternitas	Moneta
Annona	Munificentia
Bon. Eventus	Nobilitas
Caritas	Ops
Claritas	Patientia
Clementia	Pax
Concordia	Perpetuitas
Fecunditas	Pietas
Felicitas	Providentia
Fides	Pudicitia
Fortuna	Quies-Requies
Genius	Salus
Hilaritas	Securitas
Honos	Spes
Indulgentia	Tranquillitas
Iustitia	Uberitas
Iuventus	Victoria
Laetitia	Virtus

While, however, there are princes who adopted only one, others who adopted as many as thirty, some Personifications appeared under only one prince, and there are others which appeared under a hundred and twenty different rulers.

The number of the rulers who adopted Personifications is as follows : *Victoria* was adopted by 120 princes, *Concordia* 93, *Salus* 78, *Virtus* 76, *Pax* 69, *Felicitas* and *Securitas* 67, *Pietas* 66, *Fides* and *Providentia* 61, *Aequitas* 57, *Fortuna* 54, *Spes* 53, *Moneta* 47, *Aeternitas* 36, *Liberalitas* 32, *Laetitia* 31, *Libertas* 30, *Annona* 28, *Genius* 26, *Abundantia* 23, *Pudicitia* 21, *Uberitas* 20, *Hilaritas* 18, *Concordia* 16, *Indulgentia* 15, *Iustitia* 12, *Bonus Eventus* 10, *Perpetuitas* 9, *Claritas* 8, *Nobilitas* 7, *Tranquillitas* 6, *Honos*, *Iuventas* and *Quies* 5, *Munificentia* 4, *Caritas* and *Ops* 2, *Patientia* 1.

The number of the Personifications adopted by each ruler is as follows:

Antoninus Pius adopted 31, Gallienus and Hadrian 27, Septimius Severus 25, Commodus and Caracalla 24, Claudius Gothicus 23, Marcus Aurelius, Alexander Severus, Diocletian 22, Elagabalus 21, Tetricus major 20, Carinus and Maximianus Herculeus 19, Trajan, Gordianus Pius, Trebonianus Gallus, Valerianus, Postumus, Probus, Carausius 18, Vespasianus, Volusianus, Victorinus, Quintillus, Tacitus and Galerius Maximianus 17, Julia Domna, Geta, Philippus major, Salonina, Florianus, Carus, Constantius

Chlorus and Galba 16, Trajanus, Decius and Constantinus M. 15, Titus, Domitianus and Tetricus minor 14, Pescennius, Albinus, Aurelianus and Allectus 13, Vitellius, Faustina the younger, Numerianus, Crispus and Constantius II 12, Julia Mammea 11, Nerva, Lucius Verus, Macrinus, Maximinus, Philippus minor, Hostilianus and Constantinus II 10, Faustina the Elder, Herennius Etruscus and Maximinus Daza 9, Lucilla, Julia Maesa, Otacilia, Etruscilla, Æmilianus, Saloninus and Valens 8, Nero, Ælius, Pertinax, Balbinus, Maxentius and Licinius the younger 7, Crispina, Pacatianus, Macrianus, Marius, Severus II, Licinius the elder, Constans I, Valentinianus I, Gratianus and Valentinianus II 6, Augustus, Gordianus I, Gordianus II, Pupienus, Quietus, Helena, Magnentius, Constantius Gallus, Julianus II, Theodosius and Honorius 5, Sabina, Julia Soaemias, Julia Paula, Valerianus the younger, Lælianus, Vaballathus, Magnia Urbica, Fausta, Decentius, Magnus Maximus and Eugenius 4, Julius Cæsar, Marcus Antonius, Livia, Claudius, Otho, Domitilla, Plautilla, Aquilia, Tranquillina, Regalianus, Severina, Iovianus, Flavius Victor and Valentinianus III 3, Julia (daughter of Titus) Didius Julianus, Didia Clara, Plotina, Diadumenianus, Orbiana, Domitius Domitianus, Theodora, Hannibalianus, Vetranion, Procopius, Galla Placidia, Sebastianus, Priscus Attalus, Iovianus, Grata Honoria, Majorianus, Anthemius and Romulus Augustulus 2, Pompey M., Brutus, Cassius, Fulvia, Tiberius, Caligula, Nero, Drusus, Domitia, Matidia, Manlia Scantilla, Annia Faustina, Maximus, Jotapianus, Cornelia Supera, Mariniana, Saturninus, Helena, Flaccilla, Constantius III, Constantinus III., Constans (tyrant), Maximus (tyrant), Iovinus, Eudoxia, Petronius, Avitus, Severus III, Euphemia, Olybrius, Placidia, Glycerius and Julius (nephew) 1. Finally, the following did not adopt Personifications; Pompeius Sextus, Lepidus, C. Antonius, L. Antonius, Agrippa, Caius Cæsar, Drusus, Antonia, Germanicus, Agrippina the elder, Agrippina the younger, Clodius Macer, Marciana, Paulina, Dryantilla, Galeria Valeria, Romulus, Alexander (tyrant), Valens (tyrant), Martinianus, Delmatius, Vetranion, Nepotianus.

SYNOPTIC TABLE OF THE ALLEGORICAL PERSONIFICATIONS.

	Abundantia	Aequitas	Aeternitas	Annona	Bon. Eventus	Caritas	Claritas	Clementia	Concordia	Fecunditas	Felicitas	Fides	Fortuna	Genius	Hilaritas	Honos	Indulgentia	Iustitia	Iuventus	Laetitia	Liberalitas	Libertas	Moneta	Munificentia	Nobilitas	Ops	Patientia	Pax	Perpetuitas	Pietas	Providentia	Pudicitia	Quies-Requies	Salus	Securitas	Spes	Tranquillitas	Uberitas	Victoria	Virtus	
Pompey Magnus																														●											1
J. Caesar								●																						●									●		3
M. J. Brutus																						●																			1
Cassius,																						●																			1
D. Ahenobarbus																																									—
Q. Labienus																																									—
S. Pompey																																									—
Lepidus																																									—
M. Antonius									●																					●									●		3
Fulvia																																							●		1
C. Antonius																																									—
Augustus									●				●															●			●								●		5
Livia																		●												●				●							3
Agrippa																																									—
C. Caesar																																									—
Tiberius								●															●																		2
Drusus																																									—
Nero Drusus																																				●					1
Antonia																																									—
Germanicus																																									—
Agrippina Sen.																																									—
Caligula																														●											1
Claudius																					●							●								●					3

	Abundantia	Aequitas	Aeternitas	Annona	Bon. Eventus	Caritas	Claritas	Clementia	Concordia	Fecunditas	Felicitas	Fides	Fortuna	Genius	Hilaritas	Honos	Indulgentia	Iustitia	Iuventus	Laetitia	Liberalitas	Libertas	Moneta	Munificentia	Nobilitas	Ops	Patientia	Pax	Perpetuitas	Pietas	Providentia	Pudicitia	Quies-Requies	Salus	Securitas	Spes	Tranquillitas	Uberitas	Victoria	Virtus	
Britannicus																																									—
Agrippina Jun																																									—
Nero				●					●					●								●												●	●				●		7
Clodius Macer																																									—
Autonomous		●			●				●		●	●	●	●								●	●					●						●	●						12
Galba		●							●		●	●	●			●						●						●		●	●			●	●				●	●	14
Otho																												●							●				●		3
Vitellius		●		●				●	●			●				●						●						●			●				●				●	●	12
Vespasianus		●	●	●					●		●	●	●	●		●						●						●			●			●	●	●			●	●	17
Domitilla									●				●																	●											3
Titus		●	●	●	●				●		●	●	●	●														●			●			●	●				●		14
Julia									●																									●							2
Domitian		●	●	●					●		●	●	●										●					●			●			●	●				●	●	14
Domitia																														●											1
Nerva		●		●					●				●					●				●	●					●						●					●		10
Trajan	●	●	●						●		●	●	●	●				●				●						●		●	●			●	●	●			●	●	18
Plotina												●																				●									2
Marciana																																									—
Matidia																														●											1
Hadrian		●	●	●	●			●	●		●	●	●	●	●		●	●			●	●	●				●	●		●	●	●		●	●	●	●		●	●	27
Sabina									●								●													●		●									4
Ælius									●		●		●		●													●		●				●							7
Antoninus Pius	●	●	●	●	●			●	●		●	●	●	●	●	●	●	●		●	●	●	●	●		●		●		●	●	●		●	●	●	●		●	●	31
Faustina Sen.			●						●	●			●															●		●				●	●	●					9
M. Aurelius	●	●		●				●	●		●	●	●	●	●	●			●		●							●		●	●			●	●	●			●	●	22
Faustina Jun			●						●	●	●		●		●		●			●										●		●		●							11

Lucius Verus									●		●		●		●		●				●							●			●			●					●		10
Lucilla									●	●			●		●					●										●		●		●							8
Commodus	●	●		●					●		●	●	●	●	●					●	●	●	●	●	●			●		●	●	●		●	●	●			●	●	24
Crispina									●	●					●					●												●		●							6
Pertinax		●	●																	●	●		●			●					●										7
Didius Julianus									●				●																												2
M. Scantilla																														●											1
Didia Clara													●		●																										2
Pescennius			●		●				●		●	●	●					●					●							●				●		●			●	●	13
Albinus		●						●	●		●	●	●	●									●					●			●			●					●	●	13
Sept. Severus	●	●		●	●				●		●	●	●	●			●	●		●	●	●	●	●	●			●		●	●			●	●	●			●	●	25
Julia Domna		●	●						●	●	●		●		●		●			●	●		●							●	●	●			●				●		16
Caracalla	●	●		●	●				●		●	●	●				●	●	●	●	●	●	●		●			●		●	●			●	●	●			●	●	24
Plautilla									●						●															●											3
Geta		●			●				●		●	●	●							●	●	●			●					●	●				●	●			●	●	16
Macrinus	●	●		●							●	●									●										●			●	●				●		10
Diadumenianus												●																								●					2
Elagabalus	●	●	●	●					●		●	●	●		●					●	●	●		●	●			●		●	●			●	●	●			●		21
Julia Paula		●							●				●							●																					4
Aquillia Severa		●							●									●																							3
Julia Soemias		●		●							●																					●									4
Julia Maesa		●								●	●		●							●								●		●		●									8
Annia Faustina									●																																1
Sev. Alexander	●	●	●	●					●		●	●	●				●	●			●	●	●					●	●	●	●			●	●	●			●	●	22
Orbiana									●	●																															2
Mammæa	●	●		●					●	●	●																	●		●		●		●							11
Maximinus I		●									●	●					●				●							●			●			●		●			●		10
Paulina																																									—
Maximus																														●											1
Gordianus I									●																						●				●				●	●	5
Gordianus II									●																						●				●				●	●	5
Balbinus						●			●			●																●		●	●								●		7

	Abundantia	Aequitas	Aeternitas	Annona	Bon. Eventus	Caritas	Claritas	Clementia	Concordia	Fecunditas	Felicitas	Fides	Fortuna	Genius	Hilaritas	Honos	Indulgentia	Iustitia	Iuventus	Laetitia	Liberalitas	Libertas	Moneta	Munificentia	Nobilitas	Ops	Patientia	Pax	Perpetuitas	Pietas	Providentia	Pudicitia	Quies-Requies	Salus	Securitas	Spes	Tranquillitas	Uberitas	Victoria	Virtus	
Pupienus						●			●																			●			●								●		5
Gordianus III		●	●	●					●		●	●	●							●	●	●	●					●		●	●			●	●				●	●	18
Tranquillina									●		●																			●											3
Philippus I		●	●	●					●		●	●	●							●	●							●						●	●	●	●		●	●	16
Otacilia				●					●	●	●																			●		●		●	●						8
Philippus II		●	●						●		●	●									●							●								●			●	●	10
Pacatianus									●		●	●	●															●											●		6
Jotapianus																																							●		1
Trajanus Decius	●	●									●			●							●	●	●					●		●		●			●			●	●	●	15
Etruscilla	●								●	●											●											●			●			●	●		8
Herennius		●							●					●																●		●			●	●		●	●		9
Hostilianus		●							●																					●	●	●		●	●	●		●	●		10
Treb. Gallus		●	●	●					●		●		●								●	●	●					●		●	●	●		●	●			●	●	●	18
Volusianus		●	●	●					●		●		●								●	●	●					●		●	●			●	●			●	●	●	17
Æmilianus			●						●			●																●						●		●			●	●	8
Corn. Supera									●																																1
Valerianus I		●	●	●	●				●		●	●	●								●		●					●		●	●		●	●	●				●	●	18
Mariniana											●																														1
Gallienus	●	●	●	●	●				●	●	●	●	●	●			●			●	●	●	●					●		●	●	●		●	●	●		●	●	●	27
Salonina		●		●					●	●	●		●				●			●			●					●		●	●	●		●	●			●			16
Saloninus											●	●									●		●					●		●						●			●		8
Valerianus II																															●				●				●	●	4
Macrianus		●										●	●				●																			●			●		6
Quietus		●											●																	●						●			●		5
Regalianus									●													●									●										3
Druantilla																																									—

Postumus	·	·	●	·	·	·	●	·	●	·	●	●	●	·	·	·	·	·	·	●	●	●	●	·	·	·	·	●	·	●	●	·	·	●	·	●	·	●	●	●	18
Lælianus	·	·	·	·	·	·	·	·	·	·	●	·	·	·	·	·	·	·	·	·	·	·	·	·	·	·	·	●	·	·	·	·	·	·	·	·	·	·	●	●	4
Victorinus	●	●	·	·	·	·	·	·	●	·	●	●	●	·	·	·	●	·	·	●	·	·	·	·	·	·	·	●	·	●	●	·	·	●	●	●	·	●	●	●	17
Marius	·	●	·	·	·	·	·	·	●	·	●	●	·	·	·	·	·	·	·	·	·	·	·	·	·	·	·	·	·	·	·	·	·	·	·	·	·	·	●	●	6
Tetricus I	●	●	●	·	·	·	·	·	●	·	●	●	●	·	●	·	·	·	·	●	●	·	●	·	●	·	·	●	·	●	●	·	·	●	·	●	·	●	●	●	20
Tetricus II	·	●	●	·	·	·	·	·	·	·	·	·	·	·	●	·	·	·	·	●	·	·	●	·	●	·	·	●	·	●	●	·	·	●	·	●	·	●	●	●	14
Claudius Gothicus	●	●	●	●	·	·	·	·	●	●	●	●	●	·	·	·	·	·	●	●	●	●	●	·	·	·	·	●	·	●	●	·	●	●	·	●	·	●	●	●	23
Quintillus	·	●	●	·	·	·	·	·	●	·	●	●	●	●	·	·	·	·	·	●	●	●	·	·	·	·	·	●	·	●	●	·	·	·	●	·	·	●	●	●	17
Aurelianus	·	·	●	·	·	·	·	·	●	·	●	●	·	●	·	·	·	·	·	·	·	●	·	·	·	·	·	●	·	●	●	·	·	·	●	·	·	●	●	●	13
Severina	·	·	·	·	·	·	·	·	●	·	·	·	·	·	·	·	·	·	·	●	·	·	·	·	·	·	·	·	·	·	●	·	·	·	·	·	·	·	·	·	3
Vaballathus	·	●	●	·	·	·	·	·	·	·	·	·	·	·	·	·	·	·	●	·	·	·	·	·	·	·	·	·	·	·	·	·	·	·	·	·	·	·	·	●	4
Zenobia	·	·	·	·	·	·	·	·	·	·	·	·	·	·	·	·	·	·	·	·	·	·	·	·	·	·	·	·	·	·	·	·	·	·	·	·	·	·	·	·	—
Tacitus	·	●	●	·	·	·	·	●	●	·	●	●	·	·	·	·	·	·	·	·	·	●	●	·	·	·	·	●	·	·	●	·	·	●	●	●	●	●	●	●	17
Florianus	·	●	●	·	·	·	·	●	●	·	●	●	●	·	·	·	●	·	·	·	·	·	·	·	·	·	·	●	●	·	●	·	·	●	●	·	·	●	●	●	16
Probus	●	●	●	·	·	·	·	●	●	·	●	●	·	·	·	·	·	·	·	●	·	·	●	·	·	·	·	●	●	●	●	·	·	●	●	●	·	·	●	●	18
Carus	●	●	●	·	·	·	·	●	·	·	●	●	●	·	·	·	·	·	·	·	·	·	●	·	·	·	·	●	●	·	●	·	·	●	●	●	·	·	●	·	16
Numerianus	●	·	·	·	·	·	·	●	·	·	●	●	·	·	·	·	·	·	·	·	·	·	●	·	·	·	·	●	·	●	●	·	·	·	●	·	·	·	●	●	12
Carinus	●	●	●	·	·	·	·	●	●	·	●	●	●	●	·	·	·	·	·	●	●	·	●	·	·	·	·	●	·	●	●	·	·	●	●	·	·	·	●	●	19
M.ª Urbica	·	·	·	·	·	·	·	·	●	·	·	●	·	·	·	·	·	·	·	·	·	·	·	·	·	·	·	·	·	·	·	●	·	●	·	·	·	·	·	·	4
Saturninus	·	·	·	·	·	·	·	·	·	·	·	·	·	·	·	·	·	·	·	·	·	·	·	·	·	·	·	·	·	·	·	·	·	·	·	·	·	·	●	·	1
Nigrinianus	·	·	·	·	·	·	·	·	·	·	·	·	·	·	·	·	·	·	·	·	·	·	·	·	·	·	·	·	·	·	·	·	·	·	·	·	·	·	·	·	—
Julianus	·	·	·	·	·	·	·	·	·	·	●	·	·	·	·	·	·	·	·	·	·	●	·	·	·	·	·	·	·	·	·	·	·	·	·	·	·	·	●	·	3
Diocletianus	●	●	●	●	·	·	●	●	●	·	●	●	●	●	·	·	·	·	·	●	·	·	●	·	·	·	·	●	·	●	●	·	●	●	●	●	·	·	●	●	22
Maximianus Herc.	●	●	●	·	·	·	●	●	●	·	●	●	●	●	·	·	·	·	·	·	·	·	●	·	·	·	·	●	·	●	●	·	●	●	●	·	·	·	●	●	19
Carausius	●	●	·	·	·	·	·	·	●	·	●	●	●	·	●	·	·	·	·	●	●	·	●	·	·	·	·	●	·	●	●	·	·	●	●	·	·	●	●	●	18
Allectus	·	●	·	·	·	·	·	·	·	·	●	●	·	·	●	·	·	·	·	●	·	·	●	·	·	·	·	●	·	●	●	·	·	●	·	●	·	·	●	●	13
D. Domitianus	·	·	·	·	·	·	·	·	·	·	·	·	·	●	·	·	·	·	·	·	·	·	·	·	·	·	·	·	·	·	·	·	·	·	·	·	·	·	●	·	2
Constantius Chlorus	·	·	·	·	·	·	●	·	●	·	●	●	●	●	·	·	·	·	·	●	·	·	●	·	·	·	·	●	·	●	●	·	●	●	●	·	·	·	●	●	16
Helena	·	·	·	·	·	·	·	·	·	·	●	·	·	·	·	·	·	·	·	·	·	·	·	·	·	·	·	●	·	●	●	·	·	●	·	·	·	·	·	·	5
Theodora	·	·	·	·	·	·	·	·	·	·	·	·	·	·	·	·	·	·	·	·	·	·	·	·	·	·	·	●	·	●	·	·	·	·	·	·	·	·	·	·	2
Gal. Maximianus	·	·	●	·	·	·	●	·	●	·	●	●	●	●	·	·	·	·	·	●	·	·	●	·	·	·	·	●	·	●	●	·	·	●	●	·	·	·	●	●	17
Gal.ª Valeria	·	·	·	·	·	·	·	·	·	·	·	·	·	·	·	·	·	·	·	·	·	·	·	·	·	·	·	·	·	·	·	·	·	·	·	·	·	·	·	·	—

	Abundantia.	Aequitas	Aeternitas	Annona	Bon. Eventus	Caritas	Claritas	Clementia	Concordia	Fecunditas	Felicitas	Fides	Fortuna	Genius	Hilaritas	Honos	Indulgentia	Iustitia	Iuventus	Laetitia	Liberalitas	Libertas	Moneta	Munificentia	Nobilitas	Ops	Patientia	Pax	Perpetuitas	Pietas	Providentia	Pudicitia	Quies-Requies	Salus	Securitas	Spes	Tranquillitas	Ubertas	Victoria	Virtus	
Severus II									●		●	●		●															●											●	6
Maximinus Daza									●		●			●									●					●	●						●				●	●	9
Maxentius			●								●	●											●					●											●	●	7
Romulus																																									—
Alex. Severus																																									—
Licinius I									●					●																	●				●				●	●	6
Constantia																														●											1
Licinius II									●		●																				●				●	●			●	●	7
Valens tyr																																									—
Martinianus																																									—
Constantinus Magnus							●		●		●			●				●					●					●	●	●					●	●			●	●	15
Fausta																														●				●	●	●					4
Crispus							●		●		●								●				●					●			●			●	●		●		●	●	12
Delmatius																																									—
Hanniballianus											●																								●						2
Constantinus II							●				●												●								●				●	●	●	●	●	●	10
Constans I											●																							●	●	●			●	●	6
Constans II									●		●										●		●					●		●	●			●	●	●			●	●	12
Nepotianus																																									—
Vetranion																																							●	●	2
Magnentius											●										●													●	●				●	●	6
Decentius		●																																●					●	●	4
Constantius Gallus									●		●																									●			●	●	5
Julianus II																							●												●	●			●	●	5
Helena														●																											1
Jovianus																							●												●				●		3

Valentinianus I																						●					●						●	●				●	●	6
Valens																						●					●		●				●	●	●			●	●	8
Procopius																						●												●				●		2
Gratianus									●		●																		●					●				●		6
Valentinianus II									●																				●				●		●			●	●	6
Theodosius I									●																								●		●			●	●	5
Flaccilla																																	●							I
Maximus									●																										●			●	●	4
Victor																																			●			●	●	3
Eugenius																																	●		●			●	●	4
Honorius									●																								●		●			●	●	5
Constantius III																																						●		I
Placidia																																	●					●		2
Constantinus III																																						●		I
Constans																																						●		I
Maximus																																						●		I
Jovinus																																						●		I
Sebastianus																																						●	●	2
Attalus																																						●	●	2
John																																	●					●		2
Valentin. III																																	●					●	●	3
Lic.[a] Eudoxia																																	●							I
Grata Honoria																																	●					●		2
Petr. Maximus																																						●		I
Avitus																																						●		I
Majorianus																																						●	●	2
Severus III																																						●		I
Anthemius																																	●					●		2
Euphemia																																						●		I
Olybrius																																	●							I
Placidia																																	●							I
Glycerius																																						●		I
Julius Nepos																																						●		I
Romulus Augustulus																																	●					●		2
	23	57	36	28	10	2	8	16	93	13	67	62	54	26	18	5	15	12	5	31	32	30	47	4	7	2	69	I	9	66	61	21	5	78	67	53	6	20	120	76	

SKETCH OF THE ALLEGORICAL PERSONIFICATIONS WITH THEIR RELATIVE TYPES AND SYMBOLS.

ABUNDANTIA.

ABVNDANTIA AVG, AVG N, AVGG, AVGG ET CAESS N N — TEMPORVM — ALIMENTA

It is during the splendid reign of Trajan that the idea of great riches, of plenty, and of the replenishing of all life's needs, makes its first appearance upon the Roman Coinage. The legend ABVNDANTIA is still wanting, ALIM. ITAL. being used in its stead; but the female figure, holding the cornucopiæ and the ears of corn, and distributing her gifts to the sons of the people, is precisely that of Abundance, as we find her frequently with her own legend from the reign of Elagabalus until the time of the four Emperors. She is generally represented as a matron holding a cornucopiæ. (commonly called horn of plenty) and some ears of corn. Usually the figure of Abundantia is represented alone, sometimes however, and principally upon some medallions (see for example those of Julia Mammaea and Salonina), she forms part of a more complex picture and is placed between the Emperor and Minerva or with other figures. Sometimes Abundantia holds simply the cornucopiæ, sometimes she pours the contents into a modius or towards some person who receives them.

> Aurea fruges
> Italiam pleno diffundit copia cornu.
> Hor., *Ep.* 12, Lib. I.
>
> .... tipi copia
> Manabit ad plenum benigno
> Ruviis honorum opulenta cornu.
> Hor., Lib. I, *Od.* 17.

It is difficult to determine whether the cornucopiæ contained money or fruit, but I should incline to the second hypothesis although both money and the fruits of the earth lend themselves equally to the symbolizing of Abundantia.

Abundantia also at some periods was used as a representation of *Seculo frugifero*, a legend to which, under Pertinax and Postumus, a winged caduceus and ears of corn corresponded, under Albinus and Severus, the Genius of Abundance, also under the same Albinus a divinity, not yet determined, who has all the characteristics of an

African Ceres and yet must certainly be taken to signify Abundantia.

AEQUITAS.

AEQVITAS (or AEQVTAS or ECVITAS) (AEQVITATI) — AVG, AVGVST, AVGVSTI, AVGG, AVG NOSTRI — MVNDI — PVBLICA — AERES AVGVST.

Æquitas is not to be confused with *Justitia* which we also find on the Roman coinage. If the latter is to be understood in the moral sense as judgment of human actions, Æquitas must be understood in the sense of commercial economics, that which establishes the rectitude of transactions, and to which the value of the coins publicly corresponds.

Introduced by Vespasian, the personification of Æquitas lasted, with few interruptions, until Constantine, after whom she is to be found only on a silver medallion of Decentius.

Originally, Æquitas was represented by a matron standing, with a balance in her right hand and a long spear in the left which has come to be called a sceptre, but which most probably represented the measure, *pertica*, used in land surveying.

Nerva substituted for this symbol the cornucopiæ, by this change making *Æquitas* equal to *Moneta*. Indeed, the result is, that the same personification is accompanied sometimes by one legend, and sometimes by the other (vide *Moneta*) to that the two legends come to be stamped indifferently, especially on the medallions of the third and fourth centuries bearing the representations of the three *Monetae*.

In some very rare cases a palm-branch is substituted for the cornucopiæ.

On a unique middle bronze of Titus the figure of *Aequitas* with the balance and the spear is accompanied by the legend AERES AVGVST.

When the three Monetae (vide *Moneta*) are used to personify *Aequitas*, each holds the balance and the cornucopiæ, and each has at her feet a heap of metal representing gold, silver and bronze coins.

AETERNITAS.

AETERNITAS (AETERNITATI) — AVG, AVGVSTA, AVGVSTI, AVGG — IMPERII — P(opuli) R(omani) — AETERNITATIBVS.

Vespasian was the first to adopt *Aeternitas*, which lasted for three centuries, until the time of Maximianus Herculeus.

The types used to represent her are exceedingly various and numerous. The most common, and those which may be considered as true Personifications are represented by a female figure, often veiled, who carries a head of the Sun and the Moon, one in each hand, and this is therefore, so to speak, a derived symbol.

The Sun and the Moon which impassively rise and set upon the vicissitudes of human life were adopted as symbols of Eternity from the earliest times :

> Soles occidere et redire possunt
> Nobis cum semel occidit brevis lux
> Nox est perpetua una dormienda.
> Catullus.
> Damna tamen celeres reparant cœlestia lunae
> Nos ubi decidimus
> Quo Pius Aeneas, quo Tullus dives et Aneus
> Pulvis et humbra sumus.
> Hor., *Od.* 7, Lib. IV.

The globe was more especially the ancient symbol of Eternity and much more appropriate than that of our serpent swallowing its tail.

> Haec aeterna manet, divisque simillima forma est
> Cui neque principium et usquam, nec finis in ipso
> Sed similis toto remanet, perque omnia par est.
> *De rotunditate corporum.* Manil., Lib. I.

Therefore *Aeternitas* is represented on the coins as a female figure with a sceptre, seated upon a globe, or a globe surmounted by a phœnix; also by a female figure standing, with the sceptre and cornucopiæ, leaning against a column or the right foot placed on a globe.

But there are many other types, or rather symbols with which the legend AETERNITAS is united, and, principally in the reigns of the Antonines, the motto AETERNITAS, commonest upon the coins of the Empresses, is combined with the most varied representations. Not seldom we find it accompanied by the figure of Ceres, of Diana, Juno, Pietas, Fortuna, Italia, of the Augusta herself, drawn in a biga of lions or in a quadriga of elephants, sometimes by a temple, or finally, by a scene in the battle of the Romans against the Sabines on a Medallion of Faustina the elder.

In more recent times, under Maxentius and Probus, the Dioscuri and the Roman wolf correspond with AETERNITAS. If to these representations we add the signification of the different legends, as AETERNITAS AVG, the most common, AETERNITAS P(opuli) R(omani), which is found on a very rare bronze of Vespasian, AETERNITAS IMPERII, rather common on the coins of the

Severi, it will easily be seen how the fundamental conception of Eternity, or let us rather say more precisely, of Stability — for AETERNITAS is not understood in the modern or Christian sense — is always to be referred to Rome, to the Roman Empire or to the Imperial family. ROMA AETERNA is always the ultimate signification in whatever manner Eternity may be presented to us.

.... polus dum sidera pascet
Semper honos nomenque tuum, laudesque manebunt.
Virg., *En.*, Lib. I.

ANNONA.

ANNONA (ANNONAE) — AVG, AVGVSTA, AVGVSTI, AVGVSTORVM — ANNONA AVGVSTI CERES — AVGVSTI FELIX.

Although Annona has a certain and even great analogy with Abundantia — for almost exactly the same symbols represent both personifications — it is necessary to keep her distinct, and to explain fully the Roman signification, which is quite special and much more important than would be supposed by those who would judge by the ambiguity of modern habits of thought. To understand her importance we must carry ourselves back to those times when Republican Rome, not being able to produce sufficient food for her own consumption, had her granaries in Sicily and Sardinia. When these islands were no longer sufficient to feed the ever growing colossus it was necessary to have recourse to Egypt and Africa : and Tacitus observes that the Roman citizens were saddened by this necessity, thinking that their subsistence was in the power of winds and tempests. The enormous quantity of grain needed for the feeding of imperial Rome, of which one third was furnished by Italy and two thirds by Africa, was gathered into the ports under the surveillance of the Roman procurators in the ports, and from them sent to the capital where the necessary enormous granaries had been built. A special fleet was organized for its transport which sailed at fixed times, and which caused an extraordinary liveliness in the ports of Ostia and Pozzuoli, where the people gathered *en masse* to see the arrival of the great triremes which were bringing the food of Rome.

It will be easily understood from this how *Annona* (being the sustenance for one year [1]) had an extraordinary importance for the Romans and was deemed worthy of deification.

---

1. For this reason it seems to me natural that Annona should derive her name from *Annus*, while the etymology has, to me, the appearance of a play upon words, which would derive it from AD NONAM, that is to say from the ora NONA, the hour which was dedicated by the Romans to breakfast.

Annona Sancta enjoyed a special cult in the ports of departure and arrival, which owed a great part of their prosperity to her, and where many people, sailors, weighers, porters, and all kinds of workmen gained their livelihood by her. Hence it is natural that temples and altars to the goddess Annona should be erected in Rome, in which to implore abundant harvests and favourable seas, upon which two circumstances the food of the great metropolis depended.

It is for this reason that Annona is represented as a woman whose constant emblems are the cornucopiæ, the modius filled with ears of corn and fruits of the earth, and the tesserae, and, either in the foreground or the background, the prow of a trireme is never wanting. On a very rare bronze of Antoninus, where Annona has the epithet of FELIX, a lighthouse is also seen.

Annona appears on the coinage for the first time under Nero, when she is represented in company with Ceres, who completed the idea signified by the legend (ANNONA AVGVSTI CERES). She is not, however, among the more frequent commemorations which were made at intervals even to the time of Diocletian.

BONUS EVENTUS.

BONVS EVENTVS — BONO EVENTVI.

A type which occurs rarely and which, as to signification, makes, as it were, a duplicate with FORTVNA. It is represented as a nude male figure, who always holds in the right hand a patera from which he makes libation over a lighted altar, and in the left hand an oar, two ears of corn or a cornucopiæ.

This type was introduced by Galba, was used by a few Emperors and ended with Gallienus.

CARITAS.

CARITAS AVGG — MVTVA.

Affection is represented by a unique type upon a unique coin of Tetricus the elder.

A female figure, standing, with the right arm raised and extended; before her, an altar.

The legend CARITAS MVTVA is found on some coins of Balbinus and Pupienus, but the legend is accompanied merely by two joined hands, which, in other instances, is accompanied under these two same Emperors, by the legend : AMOR MVTVVS, FIDES MVTVA, PIETAS MVTVA.

CLARITAS.

CLARITAS AVG or AVGG — REIP or REIPVBLICAE.

Whether in order to identify the Emperor with the sun, or, so to say, make him its equal in splendour, the word CLARITAS is found in the time of Postumus and also the relative personification which is only a substitute for Sol himself. The type which corresponds to the legend CLARITAS is precisely that of Sol, a male figure, nude and radiate.

It was adopted by the four Emperors and then by the family of Constantine, and philologically, the term remained in our language as an adjective, if not as a substantive, until our time, although it is now falling into disuse.

CLEMENTIA.

CLEMENTIA (CLEMENTIAE) — AVG — CAESARIS — IMP GERMANICI — TEMP.

Moderation in the time of victory and mercy towards the vanquished are the two most discreet gifts of the conqueror. And it is in exactly this sense that CLEMENTIA must be understood. A first mention of Moderation and Clemency was made on two bronze coins of Tiberius, but with these few exceptions Clementia is represented first in the time of Tacitus and Probus, under whom she became very common.

The type of Clementia is not very definite. Sometimes she is represented as a woman, standing, with a branch and a sceptre: at another, as a female figure with a sceptre and leaning against a column. From the time of Probus the most common representation is that of two male figures (Jupiter and the Emperor) holding a globe between them representing the union of divine Clemency and imperial Clemency in the government of the world.

CONCORDIA.

CONCORDIA (CONCORDIAE) — AETERNA — AVG, AVGVSTA, AVGVSTI, AVGG, AVGGG, AVGVSTORVM — AVGG ET CAESS N N (or N N N N) — COMMODI — EQVITVM (or AEQVITVM) — EXERCITVS — EXERCITVVM — FELIX — IMPERII — LEGIONVM — MILITVM — PERPETVA — P(opuli) R(omani) — PRAETORIANORVM — PROVINCIARVM — SENATVS.

Concordia, to whom several temples were erected in Rome, in the largest of which the Senate often held its assemblies, is one of the most common Personifications and the most common of all in being adopted by the greatest number of Princes.

Beginning with Nero, we find her represented upon the coinage of almost all the Emperors, with very few exceptions, until the time of Honorius. Often she is to be referred to the Augusti or to the Senate; but more often to the military corporations, to the army in general, to the legions, to the prætorians and so on, among whom it was the great desire of the Emperor and the Senate that Concordia, *Martis sanguineas asperi quae cohibet manus; quae dat belligeris fœdera gentibus*, should always be maintained.

Very many are the types under which she is figured and many the emblems which have been attributed to her by force of circumstances. It might therefore be said that she is the personification for whom types and emblems are less specified than for any other, and they are taken or borrowed from those of Peace, with whom she became, as it were, confounded, or from Victory or Abundance, as if to signify that Pax, Victoria and Abundantia are elements indispensable to Concordia, or are her fruits.

And to these are added religious and military emblems when Concordia is connected with worship or the army.

Concordia, a seated or standing female figure, has for symbol, according to the occasion, the cornucopia, patera, branch of olive, sceptre, the lighted altar, ears of corn, a statuette of Spes, a flower, wheel, dove, prow of a vessel, or sometimes one, two, three or as many as six military emblems.

The imperial Concordia is sometimes represented with the Emperor or Empress who give her their hand, as in some bronze coins of Antoninus; also by two Emperors, as M. Aurelius with Antoninus the Elder, or his adopted brother Lucius Verus, and many times in the reign of Alexander, she is accompanied by Philippus or by Gallienus. The simple legend Concordia Augustorum on their medallion was replaced by the different names of the members of the imperial family who were represented on them.

Cases are not rare in which the figure is wanting, and a symbol alone represents Concordia, such as the dove, peacock, two hands joined, an altar, the standards or the legionary eagle.

FECUNDITAS.

FECVNDITAS (FECVNDITATI) — AVG, AVGG — AVGVSTA, AVGVSTAE — TEMPORVM.

This figure, eminently appropriate to the Empresses, was introduced by Faustina, the wife of Antoninus Pius, and was thenceforth reproduced by almost all the Empresses until Salonina, after whom she was adopted only exceptionally by a few Emperors, as by Gallienus and Claudius Gothicus.

She is generally represented as a woman with one or more

children, more rarely by the Earth surrounded by four children to represent the four seasons.

Fecunditas is a derivation from Juno, who was considered as the goddess of fecundity and is often represented with the same attributes.

FELICITAS.

FELICITAS (FELICITATI, FELICITATEM) — AETERNA — AVG, AVGVSTA, AVGVSTI, AVGVSTORVM — CAESARVM — DEORVM — IMPERII — IMPP, IMPERATORVM — ITALICA — PERPETVA — P, R, POPVLI ROMANI — POSTVMI — PVBLICA — REIPVBLICAE — ROMANORVM — SAECVLI — TEMPORVM (or FELICIA TEMPORA).

Felicitas is represented on the coins of almost all the Emperors and of all the Empresses beginning with Galba and continuing until Constantine. This is easily explicable when one considers that Felicitas was the ideal goal to which the Roman state aspired and that to the goddess Felicitas all the other goddesses were subordinate. And indeed, what are Abundantia, Æquitas, Concordia, Pax, Victoria, unless union in themselves of the supreme aim of the Felicitas of the Emperor and Roman people?

The emblems of Felicitas are the caduceus, the patera, the branch, sceptre, cornucopia; which are exactly those of the above-mentioned and similar deities.

The epithets which accompany the legend FELICITAS, aeterna, augusta, publica, perpetua, &c., have no need of explanation; but there is one that is singular, FELICITAS DEORVM, which we find on a rare Antoninianus of Mariniana; it is so rare that it is difficult to explain it. It may be that, being found on a posthumous coin, the *Felicitas* of the gods in having received the soul of Mariniana is intended; unless, the times being very sad in that degraded period, it meant that *Felicitas* could only be given by the gods.

FIDES.

FIDES (FIDEI, FIDEM), AVG, AVGG, AVGG ET CAESS N N — COHORTIVM — EQVITVM (or AEQVIT) — EXERCITVS, EXERCITVVM — FORTVNA — LEG — MAXIMA — MILITVM — MVTVA — PRAETORIANORVM — PVBLICA.

All social ranks are concerned with FIDES; — the Emperor, the army and the people. The common type of FIDES in a general sense is that of a female figure often draped: *et Fides albo velata panno* (Hor.), who holds two ears of corn in one hand and a basket of fruit in the other. Sometimes, however, she holds merely a cornucopia and patera, sometimes a dove and always one or more symbols when she is referred to the army. The military subject is sometimes amplified by the addition of the figures of the Emperor and some soldiers.

Fides is sometimes symbolized by two clasped right hands — *accipe da que fidem,* and between them — signifying its good fruits — there is often placed a caduceus, or some flowers, palm-branches, or two ears of corn and a poppy.

When Fides relates to things military, the right hands embrace an ensign, or a legionary eagle sometimes placed on a prow of a ship, or on a fulmen.

The representation of Fides extends from Galba to Maxentius.

FORTUNA.

FORTVNA (FORTVNAE) AVG, AVGG, AVGG N N, AVGG ET CAESS N N — DVX — FELIX — MANENS — MVLIEBRIS — OBSEQVENS — REDVX — BONA FORTVNA — FLORENS FORTVNA — FORS FORTVNA.

The Romans, given over to superstition, held especially to Fortuna, the goddess who presides over all events, over the life of men and that of the nation in that vague sense in which she may be confused with *Casus*, with *Bonus Eventus* and with *Providentia,* letting it be supposed that they placed a discreet faith in the Ciceronian saying *Vitam regit fortuna non sapientia*. Many temples were erected in Rome and in the Provinces to Fortuna under her various titles, and the statue of Fortuna must always accompany the Emperor and be placed in his bedroom : *Fortunam .... quae comitari principes et in cubiculis poni solebat* (Suetonius). Hence it is very natural that her figure should be very common upon the coinage and that she should appear without interruption from Augustus until Galerius Maximianus.

Fortuna is generally represented by a female figure standing or seated, and her emblems are the cornucopia, to which is often added the rudder of a ship, sometimes replaced by a prow or a globe, a patera and the olive-branch. Sometimes Fortuna is standing on a cippus ornamented with garlands, sometimes she holds a horse by the rein. When she is standing, a wheel is often near her, a symbol which is seldom wanting when she is represented seated.

GENIUS.

GENIVS (GENIO) — AVG, AVGVST, AVGVSTI — AVGVSTI D N — AVGVSTI PII — AVG FEL, FELIC — AVG ET CAESS N N — BRITANN — C C — CAESARIS — CIVIT(atis) NICOM(ediae) — EXERCITVS — EXERCITVS ILLYRICIANI — FEL(ix) — ILLYRICI — IMPERATORIS — L, LVG(duniensis) — POPVLI — P, R — POPVLI ROMANI — SENATVS — BONVS GENIVS IMPERATORIS.

Every individual, as well as every nation, every corporation, city and locality had in the Roman world, its own genius. Thus we find the Genius of the Emperor and of the Cæsar, the Genius of the Roman people, the Genius of the Army and the Senate, and that of various Cities.

Genius is generally represented by a male figure, nude, or clothed in a simple mantle worn over the shoulders and the modius on his head, a cornucopia on his arm, in the act of making a libation with a patera, sometimes over an altar. Rarely Genius holds a sceptre; more often he has an eagle at his feet. We find these two emblems associated with the Genius of the Roman people, the eagle on innumerable bronzes of the four Emperors; the sceptre accompanies the head of Genius on some denarii of the interregnum of Galba, which shows how democracy among the Romans was understood in quite a different sense from that which it has with our contemporaries. Sometimes Genius, when he represents the army, has one or more ensigns at his side (for example Trajanus Decius), and is wrapped in the toga when he represents the Senate as on several coins of Antoninus Pius.

The Personification of Genius appears for the first time on some bronze coins of Nero; it was most used in the time of the four Emperors and makes its last appearance upon one of those small bronzes attributed to Helena, wife of Julianus II, but this attribution is not fully proved and perhaps it should be assigned to the reign of Diocletian.

HILARITAS.

HILARITAS AVG, AVGG, AVGGG — P(opuli) R(omani) — TEMPOR.

HILARITAS has much affinity of meaning with LAETITIA but is not an exact synonym.

If it were, a polished and fastidious writer such as Cicero would not have written: *Hilaritas plenum judicium ac laetitiae fuit.* If LAETITIA is taken in the sense of pleasure or satisfaction with a deed happily accomplished, HILARITAS has rather the meaning of rejoicing, of pleasure, or gladness of heart.

The symbols that accompany these two Personifications are very various. HILARITAS is represented by a matron, who almost always bears a long palm-branch in one hand, and in the other a cornucopia, a branch of laurel, or a crown, and is often accompanied by one or two children, while, as will be seen, very different symbols characterize the Personification of LAETITIA. Beginning with Hadrian, she appears rarely until the time of Elagabalus and thence only exceptionally under the Tetrici, Carausius and Allectus.

HONOS.

HONOS (HONORI) — HONOS — HONOS ET VIRTVS.

Honos is represented in two distinct ways. On his first appearance upon the imperial coinage he is always accompanied by Valour (HONOS ET VIRTVS). Thus we find him on the bronze of Galba, Vitellius and Vespasian, where he is represented semi-nude with a long sceptre and the cornucopia, opposite to Valor represented in military dress armed with a lance and parazonium and with right foot placed upon a helmet. It appears that the association of Honos with Virtus arose from the legend (history or mere tradition?) that M. Marcellus, wishing to erect a temple to Honos and Virtus, and permission not being granted by the augurs, built two, arranged in such a manner that in order to enter the temple of Honos it was necessary first to pass through that of Virtus, as if to teach that the first could not be attained without the latter. The types of *Honos* and *Virtus* come down from republican times and also their associations.

We find the head of *Honos* represented as a youth, with flowing hair and laureated, upon denarii of the Aquileia and Durmia families, while the two associated figures form the reverse of the denarius of A. Fufius Calenus and Mucius Cordus. Later *Honos* is represented by a male figure, with toga, probably the Emperor himself, and we find him thus under Antoninus and Marcus Aurelius, after whom he ceases to appear.

Whether accompanied by Virtus or alone, *Honos* among the Romans, always has the signification of military glory and it is to be noted that HONOS is never accompanied by any adjective except that of the usual A·VG.

INDULGENTIA.

INDVLGENTIA (INDVLGENTIAE) — AVG, AVGG IN CARTH — AVGG IN ITALIAM — FECVNDA — PIA — POSTVMI AVG.

The word *Indulgentia* must be understood as a condonation of punishment or taxes, and from the coins it appears that we should hold that this last signification is the one commonly adopted.

Although such fiscal condonation was already recorded upon the coins of Galba and Nerva, as an act worthy of the imperial liberality and munificence, INDVLGENTIA was not personified until the time of Hadrian and she is then represented as a matron seated, holding a sceptre and with her right hand extended. In later times, besides the sceptre, she also holds a patera.

It is chiefly under the Severi that we find Indulgentia largely represented; and at this time the old type was almost completely abandoned to give place to two new ones. Indulgentia being referred specifically to the imperial condonations granted in Italy or Africa. In the first case she is represented by the figure of Italy seated upon a globe — in the second — as a precise signification of the remission of the impost to provide the cost of the great aqueduct from the Baghouan Mountains to Carthage which had burdened the Carthagenians from the time of Hadrian — by the goddess Cybele seated upon the back of a lion running. And, as a better illustration of the deed, some rocks are seen at the side from which issues a fountain.

INDVLGENTIA, however, is not among the legends which are shewn abundantly on the imperial coinage. I should incline, as was said above, to understand her in general as meaning a condonation of imposts and she may be interpreted in an exceptional sense as a remitting of penalties (although the fiscal meaning may also very well occur) upon the coins of Faustina junior and Salonina ; I do not include those of Julia Domna, she being a woman occupying herself seriously with all kinds of state affairs ; and indeed her coins with the legend INDVLGENTIA bear the same representation of Cybele upon the lion, as those of her husband Septimius Severus.

IUCUNDITAS.

IVCVNDITATI AVG.

This personification, which may be considered as almost synonymous with HILARITAS, and very like to LAETITIA, appears only once upon a denarius of Alexander Severus which is probably of Syrian fabric.

I have not thought fit, on this account, to include it in the synoptic list, chiefly because the type has a certain barbaric appearance and also because it corresponds so little with the subject, representing a woman seated, with globe and sceptre.

IUSTITIA.

IVSTITIA AVG, AVGVSTI — VENERABILIS.

When speaking of Æquitas we emphasized the difference which exists between her and Justitia.

The first is generally understood in an economical sense, the second in a moral sense, and the first has a much more extended use on the Roman coinage than the latter. Justitia whose name appears for the first time under the portrait of Livia, daughter of Augustus, was then introduced in her true personification by Nerva, who, by this symbol, wished to show that he indeed would compensate for the unjust acts, the vexations and arbitrary deeds of his predecessor, Domitian. She is repeated only on the very few coins of the lesser Emperors, Hadrian, Antoninus, M. Aurelius, Septimus Severus, and ceases with Severus Alexander, to reappear once more on some posthumous coins of Constantinus, upon which the title of VENERABILIS is added.

Type: a woman seated with a branch and sceptre, or patera and sceptre. Rarely, standing with the balance, and in that case we recall the single type of Æquitas, with whom, although distinct from her, there was always great affinity.

IUVENTAS.

IVVENTAS, IVVENTVS (or IVBENTVS) AVG — IVVENTA IMPERII.

Marcus Aurelius introduced IVVENTAS upon his coinage while he was Cæsar, representing her as a female figure, furnished with patera, in the act of throwing a grain of incense upon a lighted tripod.

We may say that this figure is unique on the coins of Marcus Aurelius, because, although three other Emperors, Caracalla, Claudius Gothicus and Vaballathus replaced the legend on some of their coins, it has no personification.

The denarius of Caracalla (IVVENTA IMPERII) represents the Emperor, the small bronze of Claudius and Vaballathus represent Hercules.

LAETITIA.

LAETITIA (LAETITIAE) — AVG, AVGVSTI, AVGG, AVGGG — AVG N. — FVNDATA — PVBLICA — TEMPORVM.

Laetitia, generally represented as a woman who holds a spear and ears of corn or a crown in the right hand, while with the left she leans upon an anchor or a rudder of a ship, is often represented merely by a trireme, all of them symbols which appear at once to refer to the arrival of grain from Sicily or Africa.

Laetitia would then be the expression of satisfaction for the assured distribution of provisions. She appears for the first time in the reign of Antoninus Pius and lasted until that of Galerius Maximianus.

LIBERALITAS.

LIBERALITAS AVG, AVGVSTI, AVGG AVGVSTORVM — AVG or AVGG I, II, III, IV, V, VI, VII, VIII, VIIII.

Liberalitas was one of the chief elements of the imperial power. *Panem et Circenses* were offered by the Emperor to the people to keep them friendly and in subjection, and though games were welcome, bread was a necessity. Hence it was very natural that Liberalitas should become one of the figures most popular with the masses and it appeared very often upon the coins struck to commemorate the imperial gifts.

The oldest coins with the legend LIBERALITAS are those of Hadrian, but the figure of Liberalitas is found on coins much older. Setting aside those of the Republic, and limiting ourselves to those of the Empire, the first that bore the figure of Liberalitas are the sestertii of Nero, representing the congiarium, that is to say, the whole scene of the distribution of money or provisions to the populace, and this was continued upon the similar coins of the subsequent Emperors, upon which the ideal figure of Liberalitas is placed between the regal figures of the Emperor, of the prefect of the pretorian guard, of some soldier, and the people who go up to the imper ial däis to receive the gift. The scene of the congiarium is represented variously with more or fewer people ; but the figure of Liberalitas is never wanting. *Preest congiariis omnibus.* It was only under Hadrian that the human figures disappeared (to reappear later) and the figure of Liberalitas held the field alone, gathering to herself that which was formerly called *Congiarium* and later took the name of *Largitio.* The figure of Liberalitas lasted until the time of Constantius II.

Several Emperors held more than one *Liberalitas* and then they are numbered: *Liberalitas* II, III, &c., up to VI by Severus and Geta, VII by Marcus Aurelius, VIII by Hadrian, VIIII by Antoninus Pius, Commodus and Caracalla.

The ordinary type of Liberalitas is a woman, standing, who bears a tessera or tablet in her right, and the cornucopia, sometimes double, in the left hand.

As secondary type there may be added a feminine figure in the act of pouring from a cornucopia (Antoninus Pius) a type more appropriate to *Abundantia.* Sometimes it is the Emperor himself, in a toga, who bears the tessera, thus representing *Liberalitas*, as may be seen on a denarius of the same Antoninus.

LIBERTAS.

LIBERTAS (or LEIBERTAS) — AVG, AVGG, AVGVSTA, AVGVSTI — P R — PVBLICA — RESTITVTA — SAECVLI — R XI (or XL R or XXXX R).

The personification of *Libertas,* who was well placed on the Republican coinage, is inappropriate, at least in many cases, on that of the Emperors. We find it no less frequently on the latter than the former as if they wished that the idea of the thing should supply what was wanting in the reality.

On the Republican coinage (which was then in use) the head only of Libertas is represented, bare or veiled, while on the Imperial coinage Libertas is personified as a female figure, usually with the cap and sceptre (or rather the wand), rarely with the cap and cornucopia.

With these emblems the figure is always standing. In Hadrian's time she is sometimes represented seated, and then, with the sceptre (or rod), she also holds a branch of olive, thus approaching closely to the types of *Pax* and *Iustitia,* with the understanding that *Pax* and *Iustitia* can only flourish under the rule of *Libertas.* She appeared in all her sincerity upon a denarius of the slayer of Caesar, upon which she is brutally expressed by the Phrygian cap between two daggers; we find her again, suddenly, on the coinage of Augustus who, as well as on his cistophori, gave her the title of LIBERTATIS VINDEX; then upon the first coins of Claudius who protested against the fanatical absolutism of his predecessor Caligula. Nero only promised liberty of speech, and upon his coins her head appears only once. Galba affirmed and confirmed the liberty promised by the Senate on many of his coins.

An interval followed under Titus and Domitianus when, the latter being assassinated, Liberty arose again under Nerva who *res olim dissociabiles miscuit, principatum et libertatem* ; after this she appeared at greater intervals under Trajan, Hadrian and the Antonines.

Later she made a fitful but rather frequent appearance upon the coins of several Emperors until the time of Tacitus. It may be said that the emblem of *Libertas* reappeared at the disappearance of every tyrant as if in promise of a better era.

She made a last exceptional appearance upon an Aureus of Julianus the tyrant [1].

---

1. I do not know if one ought to take account of the isolated case of Libertas, which, according to Janini, may be verified on a small bronze of Constantine II. It is a coin now unknown and cited only by that author who is too often inexact. Moreover the figure on that coin which ought to represent Libertas is only a hybrid personification bearing the attributes of Æquitas and Felicitas, the scales and the cornucopia.

MONETA.

MONETA AVG, AVGG, AVGGG[1] — AVGVSTI, AVGVSTORVM — CAESARVM — RESTITVTA — SACRA AVGG ET CAESS NOSTR SALVTARIS — VRBIS VESTRAE.

Originally the coins of Rome were minted in the temple of Iuno Moneta, from which circumstance the name *Moneta* came to mean the mint, and such, to be exact, is the meaning of MONETA.

At the time of the empire she makes her first appearance on an autonomous denarius of the time of Galba, when she is still represented, as in the era of the Republic, by the head alone and with the curious legend which remains unique MONETA SALVTARIS. The true personification was introduced by Domitian, a matron standing, who holds a cornucopia and the balance, a type which lasted unchanged, with some rare exceptions, in which she pours money from the cornucopia into the modius at her feet.

Beginning with the reign of Commodus, and always, with the very few exceptions on his Medallions, *Moneta* is represented with a triple emblem, three female figures representing the three metals, gold, silver and bronze. Each preserves the type described; that is, she carries the balance and the cornucopia, a small pile of metal being added at the feet of each figure.

The three figures of the Monetæ in these most common representations — the most common of all upon the medallions — are always facing and generally look to the left. The middle figure alone sometimes looks to the front. It is to be noted that, while the two figures looking right and left carry the balance with the arm lowered, the figure in the middle always holds it with the arm raised, which suggests that the latter with the lighter balance for the more precious metal, represents gold, while the other two represent silver and bronze. The middle figure of Moneta upon a medallion of Commodus is leaning against a pedestal, which also lends strength to the supposition that she is intended to represent the Moneta of gold.

Which of the two others represents silver and which bronze it is difficult to determine unless one attributes the honour of silver to the figure standing to the right of the *Moneta* of gold.

The personification of *Moneta* was introduced by Domitian and repeated by many Emperors and also by some Empresses, beginning with Julia Domna, and from the time of the four Emperors she took the epithet SACRA. Upon several Medallions of Diocletian, of the Maximiani and Constans Chlorus the single figure of *Moneta* stands

---

1. Miczay publishes also MONETA II AVG (Sept. Severus) and MONETAE AUG (Julia Domna); but, I have never seen it and am inclined to think it a bad interpretation.

between those of Jupiter and Hercules, and then the legend is MONETA IOVI ET HERCVLI AVGG.

Alexander Severus alone used the legend MONETA RESTITVTA; corroborated by another similar to it, RESTITVTOR MON. — But, while such legends might have had a positive meaning in regard to Nero, Aurelian, Diocletian and Licinius, they express only a pious desire in the case of Alexander Severus. Lampridius, indeed, records that Alexander having lowered the contributions of Elagabalus 30 per cent., he prepared special coins of half, a third, and even a quarter of a denarius of gold; but that when this reform was hindered by the poverty of the reserves the new coins were not circulated and were melted. No example has descended to us.

MUNIFICENTIA.

MVNIFICENTIA AVG — GORDIANI AVG.

The rare type of Munificentia was introduced by Antoninus Pius, and probably had its origin in the Games in the Circus which were celebrated with extraordinary grandeur. The type, which we may call classical, of Munificentia, is represented by a woman with regal ensigns, the sceptre and crown, with a lion at her feet. But on various bronzes of Antoninus, a lion only, or an elephant, represents her, and the elephant is repeated also on the coinage of Septimius Severus and Elagabalus. Gordianus Pius, on the contrary, represents her with a complete scene of wild animals fighting in an amphitheatre.

NOBILITAS.

NOBILITAS AVG or AVGG

Nobilitas, whether inherited through age or distinction of family, or acquired as a reward for high public offices, was held in the greatest esteem by the Romans: it is however little used upon the coinage. It did not appear until the time of Commodus and was quickly abused by Geta in whose case it is impossible to say to what kind of nobility it could refer. After Elagabalus it did not appear again until the time of Tetricus and his son, and with these it disappeared. We must note that instead of a Personification the title *nobilis* or *nobilissimus* was used and introduced for the first time by Philippus the younger as Cæsar, and by Diocletian, in whose time the legend was common, NOBILIS or NOBILISSIMVS CAESAR(N. C or NOB. C), NOBILISSIMA FOEMINA (NF), as we find upon the coins of Helena and Fausta.

Nobilitas is generally personified by a female figure with long sceptre and the palladium.

OPS.

OPI AVG — DIVINAE

A woman seated with two ears of corn in the right hand or with the sceptre and the right hand raised above her head — are we to suppose she represents the goddess wife of Saturnus or the Personification of Riches? I am more inclined for the second hypothesis: but have no serious reason for excluding the first. In any case such representation is very rare, and may be called exceptional, only appearing under Antoninus Pius (with the title of AVG) and under Pertinax (with the title DIVINA).

PATIENTIA.

PATIENTIA AVGVSTI.

The Roman *Patientia* as Le Vaillant well observes must not be understood in the Christian sense of supporting with strength and resignation the adversities of fate or the troubles of life, but rather in the sense of perseverance in carrying out difficult and troublesome work. This signification, which is derived from the representation itself of a female figure holding a sceptre, and indicating her strength of purpose with her right hand extended, is attributed to the great Hadrian upon a unique and rare denarius of whom we find this personification [1].

PAX.

PAX (or PAXS, PACI, PACE) — AETERNA — AVG — AVGVSTA, AVGVSTI, AVGG, AVGVSTORVM — EQVITVM — EXERCITVS — FVNDATA — ORBIS TERRARVM — PERPETVA — P. ROMANI — PVBLICA — VBIQVE PAX.

Daughter of Jupiter and of Themis, PAX, already honoured with temples and statues in Greece, had much greater honour among the Romans, who dedicated to her the most beautiful temple in Rome upon the Appian Way. Begun by Agrippina it was finished by the Flavii who deposited in it the rich spoils taken from the Temple at Jerusalem.

---

1. It is true that Spartianus recounts concerning the Emperor Hadrian "frigora et tempestates ita *patienter* tulit ut nunquam caput tegeret", but in spite of this assertion I do not think we ought to attribute to the patience of Hadrian the sense that we are accustomed to give to that of Job; and if it is true that Hadrian used always to go with his head uncovered we must conclude that covering it was distateful to him.

For although the Roman Empire was founded in war and maintained by war, peace was held in the highest esteem and considered as the reward of war and as a gift from the gods. So that it is not surprising that the coins upon which *Pax* is celebrated are very numerous.

A common type of *Pax,* which began with Augustus and lasted until the end of the Empire, is a seated female figure, standing or running, with a long sceptre, generally carried aslant, the branch of olive, cornucopia, caduceus, military ensign, ears of corn, the palm or crown. Sometimes *Pax* with the sceptre or olive-branch is in a swift biga, and thus we find her on the aurei of Gallienus and Probus with the legend VBIQVE PAX.

We sometimes find Pax with a torch in the act of setting fire to a heap of arms; but more often with the legend PAX, a representation which really relates to war, and of which according to the Roman feeling, it could only be the consequence.

Upon an Antoninianus of Gallienus with the legend PAX FVNDATA we see a trophy with two prisoners. Upon an aureus of Constantine with the legend PAX AETERNA AVG N are figured two women turreted, one of whom presents a crown to the Emperor, the other a victory; and upon a small bronze of the same Constantine with the legend PACIS FVND(ator) a representation of Mars the warrior, is given, who bears a trophy and drags along a prisoner. Such is *Pax* as understood by the Romans. And it is to be noted that, while *Victoria* is often accompanied, as we shall see in its place, by an epithet relating to the conquered people, Pax on the contrary is always understood in a general sense. Rome did not make peace by treaty with another nation, but granted it, after victory, to the whole world. *Pax orbi terrarum!*

To the coins recording *Pax* must be added those with the legend ARA PACIS (or simply PACIS) and shewing an altar, in connection with which Pax assumes a decidedly religious character.

With regard to this an observation of some interest is suggested by some coins of Salonina with the legend AVG(usta) IN PACE with a representation of *Pax* seated. It is a type which has given rise to long discussions; and different significations were attributed to it, among which is the noted one of De Witte, who would find in it a religious, Christian meaning, and, referring it to Pax Aeterna, would deduct from it the opinion that Salonina was converted to the new faith.

This interpretation appears, to me, strained, at least, and that of *Augusta sotto le spoglie della Pace* appears to me a rather more obvious meaning.

This latter would be also the key to the interpretation of other coins, among them, for example, some of the two Faustinas where the representation of Æternitas corresponds to the simple legend AVGVSTA. Would it not be natural to recognize that in this it was intended to represent the Augusta under the emblem of Aeternitas ?

PERPETUITAS.

PERPETVITAS (or PERPETVETAS, PERPETVITATI, PERPETVITATE) AVG, AVGG — IMP AVG.

There is one personification which may almost be confused with AETERNITAS. In the beginning indeed, when it was introduced by Alexander Severus, the type was a woman with sceptre and globe leaning her elbow on a column, while in later times she was replaced by the figure of Roma Nicephora (that is, holding a figure of Victory) a type used commonly to represent *Aeternitas,* and Aeternitas is precisely the *Perpetuitas* of Rome.

And it is to be noted, as in the last instance, that when Rome is represented by it, as on a bronze of Severus II and on other similar coins of Constantine, the legend PERPETVITAS is in the nominative case while upon the coins bearing the allegorical representation of *Perpetuitas* the legend referring to it is sometimes in the dative, but more often in the ablative.

Another nominative case has been verified on a denarius, belonging to Valentinianus II. On this denarius (reported by Cohen in the *Numismatic Chronicle*) with the legend PERPETVETAS we find a representation of Phœnix with the globe which also shows how Perpetuitas may be confounded in a certain manner with Aeternitas.

Perpetuitas is not one of the common types of the Roman coinage.

PIETAS.

PIETAS (PIETATI) — AETERNA, AVG, AVGG — AVGVSTA, AVGVSTAE, AVGVSTI, AVGVSTORVM — AVGG ET CAESS NN — DDD NNN — FALERI — MILITVM — MVTVA — PVBLICA — ROMANA — SAECVLI — SENATVS.

Roman piety unites in one whole, reverence for the gods, devotion to the Emperor, affection between the Augusti or between the Augustus and the people, tenderness of parents to sons, respect or affectionate care of the latter for their parents [1], and in general, love of one's neighbour, or in one word Religion. It therefore formed

---

1. Manius Acilius Glabrio erected a temple to Pietas in Rome to that young woman who nourished her old father in prison, a legend which under the name of " Roman Piety " formed the subject of a famous picture by Andrea del Sarto.

a great part of Roman political life, and wise rulers of the people held tenaciously to the preservation of such an indispensable element of government. On this account the representation of Pietas is one of the first in importance that the Empire inherited from the Republic, and, as the Emperors adopted, from the time of Augustus, the title of PIVS we find that the representation of *Pietas* is jealously and abundantly preserved upon the coinage almost without interruption until the end; relating sometimes to the Emperors, the Empresses, or Imperial families, sometimes to the senate, the army, to Rome or to the people in general.

The types of *Pietas* are : a matron occasionally seated but almost always standing and often veiled, with a patera and sceptre; very seldom with military ensigns when it refers to the army. She often stands near an altar upon which she sometimes pours from a patera or places incense. Sometimes she raises one hand or both to the sky. Finally her personification resembles that of *Fecunditas* having three or four children in her arms or near her.

Sometimes there is a temple which symbolizes Pietas or simply the instruments of sacrifice, which is easy of explanation; but the case also occurs in which the legend *Pietas* is found with the representation of Mercury — and not in error, as it is repeated many times — a combination of which it is not easy to give the precise meaning, except that in this case it may be that Mercury should not be regarded as a messenger but as a mediator between humanity and divinity.

Under Balbinus and Pupienus, the two right hands joined which have the legend CARITAS MVTVA, FIDES MVTVA and AMOR MVTVVS, have also PIETAS MVTVA.

PROVIDENTIA.

PROVIDENTIA PROVIDENTIAE — AVG, AVG N, AVGVSTI, AVGG — CAESS — DEORVM — PROBI AVG NOSTRI — SENATVS

Divine *Providentia*, among the Romans is often united and confounded with the Imperial, or rather, it begins with the aureole of divinity and becomes imperial by degrees. The legend PROVIDENTIA was introduced for the first time upon the senatorial coinage of Augustus, accompanied by the representation of a lighted altar and thus we find it also upon the coins of Vitellius, Vespasian and his sons.

Under Titus however the representation was altered and underwent a first change of meaning. Here are the two Emperors, Titus and Vespasian facing, the one presenting the other with a globe. With Trajan the personification of Providentia assumes its true character and is represented by a female figure with sceptre, often leaning against a column, and with a globe at her feet, to which she, often, points with a rod. This is the type found most often on the coinage of a great number of Emperors until the time of Constantine; this type however did not prevent other types from gradually being substituted for it, or, at any rate, modifying it.

Under Hadrian, Providentia appears to have referred still almost exclusively to the gods, so much so that on some coins she takes the title of PROVIDENTIA DEORVM, with the representation of the Emperor, in a toga, receiving a sceptre brought to him by an eagle, and therefore, evidently, *ab Jove*. The same legend, in the time of Antoninus, accompanies the representation of a fulmen, another symbol of Jupiter.

But in the reign of Commodus, Providentia descends from Olympus, and becoming earthly, is to be referred to the grain which the Emperor has brought from Africa, is almost confused with Annona, is represented now by a trireme, now by Africa herself who comes into contact with Hercules; and it is impossible to say whether, henceforth, she is related more closely with divinity or with the Emperor. The symbols and emblems are gradually modified.

For the sceptre and globe which, from the beginning, formed the true type of Providentia, are gradually substituted a cornucopia, patera, plough, ship's rudder, two ears of corn or a military ensign. Septimus Severus and Caracalla represent Providentia with the head of Medusa, Gallienus with Mercury, Aurelianus with Venus, Crispus and Constantine II with Jupiter, and the gate of a camp with which Constantius II represented her for the last time.

Providentia Deorum who first appeared upon the coinage was transformed in the course of time into *Providentia Senatus, Providentia Caess, Providentia Probi aug. nostri.*

PUDICITIA.

PVDICITIA (PVDICITIAE) — AVG, AVGG, AVGVSTAE

Pudicitia was represented for the first time on the coins of the virtuous Plotina, upon a beautiful denarius of gold and silver which bore the inscription ARA PVDIC. And the allusion was fully justified, recording as it does one of the many virtues of her who was certainly one of the best of the Empresses.

But Hadrian and Sabina adopted the same emblem immediately afterwards; in spite of the fact that the latter, who was not happy in her marriage nor probably very virtuous, had her sleep troubled by the apparition of Antinous. And then she was adopted not only by the few Empresses who could honour themselves thus, but also by the many others by whom she could not be named except ironically.

According to our modern ideas Pudicitia may be called a virtue more strictly feminine than masculine and should be adopted — whether rightly or wrongly — only by the Empresses, and hence it is strange to see it figured also upon the coins of several Emperors. If it merely concerned Trajanus Decius; Erennius Etruscus, Hostilianus, Trebonianus Gallus and Gallienus [1], we might be tempted to suppose that their coins with this impression were hybrids made with the coins of Etruscilla for the first and of Salonina for Gallienus : which would not occasion much wonder seeing how irregular the system of coinage was at this time. But we have the denarii of Hadrian (even of Hadrian himself!) which leave no doubt on the subject. There are many of his denarii upon which Pudicitia appears, and among the others there is one, which, with the same representation and the legend PVDIC in the field, bears the circular legend PM TR P COS III, which can only refer to Hadrian, this not being the age of incorrect legends.

We must therefore take as regular all the coins of the Emperors quoted above although we cannot succeed, except up to a certain point, in deciding their true signification.

Pudicitia is represented by a woman standing or seated, generally with a sceptre, draped in her own clothes, often in the act of covering with a veil her face or breast, or with her hand on mouth or breast. Sometimes she has with her one or more children, sometimes she is in the act of sacrificing upon an altar. Her figure is always alone upon the coins; but upon some rare medallions Pudicitia is accompanied by Felicitas, Securitas or Abundantia.

Upon a large bronze in my collection found last year in Rome [2] and which I believe to be unique, of Faustina the Younger with the legend PVDICITIA, the figure is seated and veiled holding two ears of corn. Probably it is intended to represent Pudicitia under the appearance of the chaste Ceres.

QUIES — REQUIES.

QVIES AVG, AVGG, AVGVSTORVM — REQVIES OPTIMORVM MERITORVM.

Two types, almost synonymous, uncommon, and differently represented.

---

1. I pass by two denarii, one barbarous and the other blundered, of Septimius Severus and Gordianus which cannot be used as data upon which to form a judgment.

2. See *Appunti di Num. Romana*, n. LXVII.

A woman standing with an oar lowered and a sceptre represents Repose, which is also represented by the Emperor seated in the curule chair, with the right hand raised and with the sceptre.

In the first case she is called QVIES and is adopted by Diocletian and Maximianus Hercules; in the second she is called REQVIES and adopted by Claudius Gothicus, Maximianus Hercules and Constantius Chlorus.

SALUS.

SALVS (SALVTI) AVG, AVGG, — AVGG ET CAESS NN — AVG NOSTRI — AVGVSTA — AVGVST — DD NN AVGG ET CAESS — DD NN — EXERCITVS GEN (or GENERIS) HVMANI — ITAL — MILITVM — POSTVMI AVG — PROVINCIARVM — PVBLICA — REIPVBLICAE.

Salus, also, is one of the very old representations, and the Empire only continued the use already introduced by the Republic.

The head only of Salus was represented for the last time by Livia, daughter of Augustus; then, under the first Emperors, the true Personification was adopted, consisting of a feminine figure standing, seated or leaning against a column, who in most cases is feeding a serpent which is sometimes placed in her arms, sometimes hangs from an altar or a tree. In other cases the figuration is less precise and the emblems are those belonging to other Personifications and especially to Pietas, such as the patera poured upon a lighted altar, perhaps to signify that Salus is a gift of the gods. The rudder of a ship and the ears of corn which are sometimes emblems of Salus evidently refer to Annona, as the first element of health.

Sometimes, also, Salus is represented by an altar. Sometimes it is Aesculapius who represents her, and here the signification is very clear.

But Salus which is mostly understood in the material sense of physical health, to which the Romans very rightly gave immense importance — *mens sana in corpore sano* — which is proved by some coins minted in memory of the restoration to health of the Emperors, is sometimes or may be understood in a metaphorical sense. Such is SALVS GENERIS HVMANI represented generally by a Victory, SALVS EXERCITVS or MILITVM, SALVS PROVINCIARVM of Postumus to which the figure of Rhenus corresponded, in which cases it cannot be determined precisely whether the concrete or the metaphorical sense is to be understood.

The word SALVS is used to express a wholly abstract meaning when in modern times, SALVS MVNDI is written round the symbol of the cross, upon an aureus of Olybrius.

SALVS is among the commonest personifications upon the Imperial coinage.

SECURITAS.

SECVRITAS (SECVRITATI) AVG, AVGG, AVGVSTI — IMPERII — IMP GERMAN (Vitellius) — ORBIS — PERPETVA — POPVLI ROMANI — PVBLICA — REIPVBLICAE — ROMAE — SAECVLI — TEMPORVM.

Securitas, another of the most frequently adopted Personifications, began, egotistically, we may say, with Nero, upon whose coins it is always written clearly with full lettering SECVRITAS AVGVSTI, while on those of Galba it always refers to the people, SECVRITAS P ROMANI. Later it was adopted by a large number of Emperors, and refers sometimes to the Emperors, sometimes to the Roman people, sometimes to the whole earth. The types are very various, but the most common is that of a woman standing or sitting in the attitude of repose of one who has nothing to fear. Provided with sceptre, patera or cornucopiæ, a crown, palm or globe, the matronly figure stands leaning against a column with the legs crossed, the right hand raised above the head, or is seated with the elbow leaning on the back of her chair in the act of supporting the head. Often near her an altar, against which a torch often leans.

Securitas almost equals Pax and is sometimes represented by Pallas (Caracalla); at other times the legend is SECVRITAS with a representation of the Emperor in a quadriga with a branch of laurel (Licinius the elder).

In the time of Constantine *Securitas* was again confounded with *Pax* but always after a Victory, and we then find the Emperor represented in the act of erecting or crowning a trophy.

Upon the middle bronzes of Julian the Apostate we find, with the legend SECVRITAS REIPVBLICAE, the representation of a bull which strongly recalls the *Bull Apis* or with greater probability a victim for sacrifice. And upon a small bronze of Hannibalianus a figure of the Euphrates is represented with the legend SECVRITAS PVBLICA.

SPES.

SPES (SPEI) — AVG, AVGG, AVGGG — AVGVSTA, AVGVSTI, AVGVSTOR — FELICITATIS ORBIS — P R — PROBI AVG — PVBLICA — R P, REIPVBLICAE — BONA SPES, BONAE SPEI — SPES FIRMA.

He who devotes himself to great works must, necessarily, be animated by the hope of success. Hope was indispensable to the Romans and was therefore placed among the divinities. Claudius introduced her upon the coinage and she remained there until the end of the Empire, her type being preserved with great regularity; a young girl in ungirdled robe, carrying a flower (symbol of hope because from the flower comes fruit)[1] in the act of walking and holding up her dress.

Upon some coins of Hadrian SPES P R, represented as just described, appears to allude to the new Caesar, whom the old Emperor, still living, presents as his successor and hope of the Roman people.

This allusion has been suggested, and, I may say, confirmed by the fact that some of these coins and especially some bronze, certainly coined in the last years of Hadrian, and with the name of Hadrian, already present the portrait of Antoninus Pius.

Sometimes Spes is in the presence of the Emperor and some soldiers (Vespasian, Alexander Severus).

In one very rare case the young girl is replaced by a male figure in the same attitude (Alex. Severus). Very rare also is the case of a temple (Herennius), with the legend SPES PVBLICA, which we must suppose to have been erected to Spes.

In the time of Constantine, the signification of Spes changed with the change in beliefs and religion. Christian Hope took the place of Pagan Spes, and the labarum with the monogram of Christ served her as symbol. In later times she was assigned the anchor as a symbol of Hope; but this symbol is not only Christian but very modern, as it does not appear upon any Imperial coinage.

TRANQUILLITAS.

TRANQVILLITAS AVG, AVGG — BEATA.

It is not a common type. Of the six Emperors who adopted it, the two first, Hadrian and Antoninus Pius, considered TRANQVILLITAS almost exactly the same as Securitas, and, indeed, represented her as a matron standing, sometimes turretted and with a sceptre, or with a rudder and two ears of corn, leaning, exactly like Securitas, against the trunk of a column. With Philippus the elder and Tacitus, Tranquillitas is represented, like Felicitas, with a dragon and the sceptre; finally, with the sons of Constantinus, Beata Tranquillitas assumed a religious character and is symbolized by a lighted altar, with a votive inscription, upon which rests a globe with three stars above.

---

1. Instead of a flower it might be a species of trefoil, the first leaves as it were torn from the stem; which, in some way, would correspond to our Italian saying "verde della Speranza" (green of hope). Indeed green must be the typical colour of Hope; it is so to-day and was so in olden times, the fresh and abundant verdure being a presage of an abundant harvest.

But this could not be realized by a coin type.

UBERITAS.

VBERTAS (or VBERITAS sometimes also VERITAS) — AVG, AVGG — SAECVLI

The Personification of Fertility of the earth did not make its first appearance upon the coinage until the time of Trajanus Decius, and lasted, intermittently, until that of Constantine. It is symbolized by a woman holding a cornucopia is her left hand and in the right an indistinct object in which many see a purse, but which it seems more reasonable to interpret as a bunch of grapes, or, perhaps, as a cow's udder as Cavedoni thought. In fact certain coins of Carausius bearing this legend correspond to this last interpretation (of this indistinct object) their type being a cow milked by a woman and this is perhaps what the barbarous Carausius meant, who, as we have observed before disregarded the mint laws and did not apply the legends rightly [1].

VICTORIA.

VICTORIA (VICTORIAE) — AVG, AVG NOSTRI, AVGG, AVGG NN (or NOSTRORVM) AVGG ET CAESS NN — DD NN AVGG. AVG I, II, III, VI, VII, VIII, VIIII — AVGVSTORVM CAESS, CAESS NN, BEATISSIMORVM CAESS — AETERNA — COMES AVG — EXERCITVS — FELIX — IMPERII ROMANI. — IVST. AVG — LAETA — LEG(ionum) LIBERA — MAXIMA — NAVALIS — PERPETVA — PRINCIPVM — BRITANNICA — CARPICA — GALLICA — GERMANICA — G(ermanica M(axima) — GOTHICA — PARTHICA — PARTHICA MAXIMA — PERSICA PONTHICA — SARMATICA — ALEXANDRI AVG N — ANTONINI AVG — CONSTANT AVG (Constantius Chlorus) CONSTANTINI AVG — CONSTANTINI CAESS — CRISPI CAES — GALLIENI AVG — GORDIANI AVG — IMP GERMANICI (Vitellius) IMP VESPASIANI — MAXIMINI AVG — OTHONIS — PROBI AVG — SEVERI AVG.

Victoria is generally represented by a female figure semi-nude and winged, in several attitudes; standing, seated upon a breastplate or some shields, in the act of walking, running, or flying, or in a biga or swift quadriga, and her attributes are a palm-branch crown, garland, sceptre, branch of bay, shield, standard or trophy. Sometimes she stands crowning a trophy, or writing upon a shield words describing a victory or offerings. Often, one or two prisoners are to be seen at her feet, or she may hold one herself by his hair. Sometimes Victoria offers a crown to the Emperor, or crowns him,

---

1. In fact this very legend Uberitas is found upon coins of Carausius with other types; for example, with that of a woman giving her hand to a soldier, which scene, apparently, has very little to do with fertility.

or precedes his horse or leads his triumphal quadriga, or accompanies him, crowning him, upon the same car.

It is not rare to find two Victories erecting a trophy or in the act of lifting a shield or of hanging it upon a palm. Upon some coins three Victories are represented. Upon a medallion of Constantine a ship is represented.

It is very natural that Victoria should furnish one of the most copious, varied, and continuous series to the Roman coinage, and such is the fact.

She figures upon it very often from the beginning of the Empire until its end, following the common law according to which the true signification, grand and real at the beginning, lessens gradually until it becomes nothing but ironical.

The glorious name Victoria, already personified, is represented in a series in the Republican epoch, assumes the greatest importance under the first Emperors and is accompanied by very varied epithets. Victoria is called *justa*, *lieta*, *libera*, *perpetua*, *maxima*, was many times placed together with the name of the countries or people conquered, and thus took the name *Britannica*, *Carpica*, *Persica*, *Gothica*, and so on, and she is identified with many expeditions, when she unites with her own the name of the victorious Emperor and becomes Victoria of Otho, of Antoninus, of Alexander, of Constantine, and others.

But the series of Victoria on the coinage was continued far beyond the age of Constantine, when the Roman world began to break up, when the barbarians by degrees invaded the empire, when, finally, the name Victoria had no meaning for the Romans. There is no Emperor who has not inscribed Victory upon his coins, and as the height of irony she also figures without any distinction upon all the coinage of the Empresses! It is also true, however, that the types were changed to be in harmony with the times.

No more crowns, no more palms, no more arms and trophies; the wretched Victoria of these times was content to replace all those with the mild and peaceful symbol of the cross!

VIRTUS.

VIRTVS (VIRTVTI, VIRTVTE) — AEQVITVM (or EQVITVM) — AETERNA — AVG, AVGG, AVG N, AVGGG, AVGG ET CAESS — AVGVSTORVM, AVGVSTORVM NN — CAESARIS, CAESARVM — CARI AVG, CARI INVICTI AVG — CLAVDI AVG — CONSTANTINI CAES — DN CONSTANTINI AVG — FALERI (VALERI?) — GALLIENI AVG — HERCVLI CAESARIS (Constantius Chlorus) — HERCVLIS (Maximianus) — POSTVMI AVG — PROBI AVG — EXERCITVS, EXERCITI, EXERCITVVM — EXERCITVS GALL — EXERCITVS ROMANI, ROMANORVM — ILLIRICI — INVICTI AVG — MILITVM — MILITVM DD NN — PERPETVA.

Upon some coins of gold and silver (Galba, Gallienus, &c.) the head of Valour is represented with the helmet like that of the young Jupiter. But this is a return to the antique republican usage.

A soldier with spear and shield or sword, generally with the right foot upon a helmet, is the most common and typical representation of Valour, who takes a great part in the representations which illustrate the whole series of Imperial coinage. The soldier, however, is often replaced by Mars or Roma in military costume and the latter stands afoot or is seated on a cuirass or some arms, always with the foot resting on a helmet which serves as foot-stool.

The personification of Valour was introduced by Galba and lasted until Constantine and beyond.

At the beginning Valour was more often represented alone and with the simple types described above and with many others more complex, Mars in all guises, with trophies and prisoners, the Emperor on foot or on horseback in the array of triumph, victory or battle, now in the act of attacking one or more enemies, now of slaying wild beasts, Romulus walking with spear and a trophy, Hercules in his different rôles, Vulcan and Minerva, a Victory who crowns the Emperor, a trophy, a lion, are all representations which illustrate the legend VIRTVS.

For the last, that is, from the beginning of the reign of Postumus, a new illustration of Valour was adopted without any special configuration.

Upon very many coins of the third century, whatever the representation of the reverse may be, we find on the obverse the legend VIRTVS POSTVMI, VIRTVS FLORIANI, VIRTVS PROBI. The idea of Valour was thenceforth identified with the name of the Emperor. Her personification was merged in that of the Emperor himself.

PART III.

THE IMPERIAL RECORDS.

The types referring to Imperial deeds which represent about a third of the whole coinage are those relating to the Emperor and his family, to the city of Rome, and to other cities and provinces, to votive offerings, games, sacrifices, to public monuments, and public events, to everything in fact which is outside the sphere of the divinities.

Among this great number of types there are some, very clear, that can be easily classified; but there are also many which are interwoven and almost confounded, either with each other, or with some given in the first two parts of this work, so that a synoptical sketch such as has been given of those here becomes absolutely impossible.

However, in order to systematize this third part in a harmonious and symmetrical manner with the two first, and to bring the work as proposed to an end, a work, we believe, let me repeat it, synthetic and embryonic, we have attempted, in spite of the extreme difficulty, a classification also of these last types, dividing them in several categories, every one of which might deserve a monograph.

I

THE EMPEROR.

A. — *The Allocutions to the Army.*

ADLOCVTIO — ADLOCVT AVG, AVG N AVGVSTI, AVGVSTORVM, COH, COH PRAETOR, MAXENTI, MILITVM — FIDES EXERC — FIDEI MILIT.

The Emperor is generally represented in military uniform; but sometimes also in a toga (Nerva) standing upon a stage, accompanied as usual by the prefect of the prætorium, or by two prefects, with a following of personages, whom to-day we should call, in modern language, his staff officers, standard-bearers carrying ensigns and standards, in the act of haranguing a certain number of pretorians or legionaries.

The allocutions took place on solemn occasions, when, for example, the Caesar had attained the purple, when the Emperor adopted a successor, who then appeared upon the scene, when he was about to set out on an expedition or returned victorious, the latter being indicated by prisoners who are seen bound and lying near the Imperial platform, when he inspected the military camps or reviewed a body of troops.

The same scene is sometimes accompanied by the legend FIDES MILITVM instead of the more common ADLOCVTIO.

The type was introduced by Caligula and lasted at intervals until Maxentius. It is usually found on the medallions of bronze and silver and on the large bronze. Rather rarely it is found upon middle bronze and upon coins of silver and gold.

B. — *The Congiaria.*

CONG AVG — CONG AVG I (or PRIMVM), II (or SECVND), III (or TERTIVM), IIII, VIII, CONG DAT POP (or P.R.) — CONG P.R. — LIBERALITAS (or LIB) AVG, II, to VIII — LIBERALITAS AVGVSTOR — LARGITIO.

It is known that solemn occasions, such as an election, the occasion of a great Victory, or important anniversaries, such as feasts, games, &c., were the best opportunities that the emperor had of gaining the favour of the populace by gifts of food and money. This was exactly the object for which the congiaria were designed. The gifts were made in kind, in money or in tesserae worth a fixed sum or a fixed measure of grain or other produce.

This distribution was made or at least inaugurated by the emperor in person and it is exactly this scene that is reproduced on the coins.

The type was introduced by Nero, but later, although the same representation was retained it assumed the title of *Liberalitas* from the time of Hadrian, and of *Largitio* about the time of the Constantines. The word *Congiarium* appears for the last time on a bronze of Septimius Severus. The scene is composed of the Emperor seated upon a platform accompanied by various personages in the act of making a distribution of bread and money to the people, often represented by one or more individuals who mount the steps of the platform with the assistance of *Liberalitas*, who presides at all the distributions. In the background is often seen the figure of Minerva, who had introduced the cultivation of the olive to the world.

It frequently happens however that this complex representation is replaced by the single figure of *Liberalitas*, who, with her emblems of the tessera and cornucopia, gathers together and represents the signification of the ceremony.

In either case, the coins with these types have become identified with those formerly attributed to Liberalitas, in the Part relating to allegorical personifications, thus forming a duplication.

C. — *Departures or Arrivals or State Entries into Cities.*

EXPEDITIO AVG — PRO, PROF, PROFECTIO AVG (or AVGVSTI), AVGG — ADVENTVS AVG — AVGVSTI — AVG N AVGVSTOR — AVGVSTORVM — CARAVSI — CARI — PROBI — S D N AVG — ADVENTVI FELICISSIMO.

The Emperor who sets out for war or returns from it victorious, or who makes his first entrance into a city is represented alone, on horseback, preceded by Victory winged and bearing the crown and palm-branch, and followed by one or more soldiers with standards, eagles and military ensigns.

The type begins with Trajan and ends with Aurelianus.

D. — *Victories and Triumphs.*

VICTORIA (see Personifications) TRIVMPHVS AVG CAESARVM — TRIVMPHVS PARTHICVS — QVADOR — TRIVMFATOR GENTIVM BARBARVM.

The Emperor is represented either on horseback fighting one or more enemies, or in a quadriga or triumphal car drawn by six horses or by elephants, crowned by Victory, accompanied by a few soldiers with palms, eagles or standards. But all these legends are often confounded with those that are accompanied by the legend *Victoria* and for that reason they may be referred to the Personifications.

E. — *Imperial Journeys through the Provinces of the Empire.*

ADVENTVI AVG AFRICAE, ALEXANDRIAE, ARABIAE, ASIAE, BITHYNIAE, BRITANNIAE, CILICIAE, GALLIAE, HISPANIAE, ITALIAE, IVDAEAE, MACEDONIAE, MAVRETANIAE, MOESIAE, NORICI, PARTHIAE, PHRYGIAE, SICILIAE, THRACIAE.

These have their greatest vogue under Hadrian. All the provinces of the Empire were visited by the great and diligent Emperors and their memory is preserved by a splendid series of coins in all the metals.

The type of these coins consists of the figure of the Province, with its own attributes, in the act of giving welcome to the Emperor.

F. — *Happy Events in the Imperial Families.*

FECVNDITAS (see Personifications) ADOPTIO CONCORDIA AVG, AVGVSTORVM (see Personifications) EQVESTER ORDO PRINCIPI IVVENT — EQVIS ROMANVS, PRINCIPI IVVENTVTIS — PONT, PONTIF, PONTIFEX MAX — SVMMVS SACERDOS AVG, AVGVR, CONSVL, COS II to XVII — CENS, CENSOR POT — PROCESSVS CONSVLARIS — TR P, TRIB POT or POTEST, II to XXXVIII — S P Q R OB CIVIS SER, SERV, SERVATOS (OB C.S.) — CONSECRATIO or AETERNITAS.

Among these are reckoned those propitious events relating to the Emperor or his family, such as births, betrothals, assumption of high office, honours, and consecrations. Births of princes are often confounded with *Fecunditas* and they are represented by her personification accompanied by one or more children, or by the Empress herself with her progeny, as in the case of Faustina the Younger, represented with her children (PVELLAE FAVSTINIANAE).

The nomination of the young princes to the Equestrian order and to the dignity of Principi Iuventutis have for their type the Caesar in military dress with the globe and staff or little sceptre.

The Adoption is represented by the Emperors with the adopted princes; promotions to the rank of Caesar, the various consulships and the different tribunal powers have no special type, but are simply mentioned in the legend.

Elections to augurships have the lituus as symbol, those to the High Pontificate the instruments of sacrifice, the præfericulum, the axe, the aspergillum or sprinkler.

*

It may be added that the coins of many princes reproduce the statues dedicated to the princes themselves, and thus, for example, the memory of the equestrian statues of Augustus, Trajan, Antoninus Pius and others is preserved to us.

The conferring of the civic crown is represented by the crown itself, in the centre of which is the legend S P Q R OB CIVIS SERVATOS or S P Q R OPTIMO PRINCIPI. The religious services of the Senate, and of the people for the Emperor on New Year's Day, are either inscribed in a crown, or are represented by branches of laurel presented to the Emperor.

Finally, the ceremony of consecration is recorded on the coins of thirty Emperors, Caesars, or Empressess, by a funeral pyre, or by a car drawn by elephants, by a funeral carriage, by peacock or eagle bearing the Empress to heaven, and always accompanied b the legend CONSECRATIO or AETERNITAS.

G. — *Other Representations of the Emperors.*

There remain many other representations of the figure of the Emperors which it is impossible to include in the categories given here, but which are not less solemn and important. The Emperor is many times represented alone or with other personages. Sometimes he is in toga or in military costume with the symbols of power, the globe and sceptre; the legend either signifies the burden of office or is a synthetic apotheosis in one word or phrase such as; SVMMVS SACERDOS, SACERDOS DEI SOLIS ELAGABAL, RECTOR ORBIS, RECUPERATOR VRBIS SVAE, RESTITVTOR REIP, ROM, VRBIS, ORBIS, SAECVLI, LIBERTATIS. Sometimes the Emperor is found with Jupiter, Roma, Fortuna or other Personifications, or with a Province to which he brings help, and we have the beautiful legends: RESTITVTORI HISPANIAE, ITALIAE; or RESTITVTORI or LOCVPLETATORI ORBIS TERRARVM; with the Senate and the legend PATER SENATVS.

It is not necessary to add that many of these types are interwoven with others already described or about to be described.

H. — *Memorial Coins.*

We may add to the coins relative to the Imperial family all the Memorial coins, that is to say, those dedicated to other living members of the Imperial family, the posthumous coins and those of restitution.

At the beginning of the Empire the custom of representing upon the coins the figure of some member of the Imperial family was inaugurated.

Augustus placed on them his daughter Julia, Tiberius Livia, Caligula his three sisters, Nero Agrippina, Trajan Plotina; Marciana Matidia, Hadrian his wife Sabina, and the Empresses appear, it may be said, regularly in a whole series too long to be enumerated.

Posthumous coins are those coined by a Prince in memory of a Prince immediately preceding him, preserving his name in sign of reverence as if to continue the first coinage before beginning his own; as Augustus had coined his first money in honour of the illustrious Julius, so Caligula, after the death of Augustus, continued to coin money with the name and head of Augustus (DIVVS AVGVSTVS PATER) and the custom, if not general, is frequent.

To these follow the coins dedicated to deceased relatives; thus Trajan put the head or figure of his father upon his own coins (DIVO TRAIANI PATRI), Hadrian dedicated some coins to his mother-in-law Matidia (DIVAE MATIDIAE SOCRVI), to his relatives Trajan and Plotina (DIVIS PARENTIBVS) and so on.

Coins of restitution are re-issues of coins coined by Princes of past times, coins reproduced precisely like their prototypes to which have been added the name of the Emperor who restores them and the word RESTITVIT (or REST).

But all these coins are memorials and signs of reverence for preceding Emperors, or for members living or dead of the Imperial family, and the coins of consecration of which we spoke above might have been placed with them.

II

THE SENATE.

CONCORDIA SENATVS — CONSENSV SENATVS — GENIO SENATVS — PATER SENATVS — PATRES SENATVS — PIETATI SENATVS — PROVIDENTIA SENATVS — SENATVS — SENATVS PIETATI AVGVSTI.

Distinguished by the senatorial sign S C which is found upon all the bronze coins of the first two centuries of the Empire, with the single exception of the small quantity coined directly by the Emperors, the Senate is nevertheless specifically indicated upon a certain number of coins. Needless to say, the Senate is represented by a Senator in a toga, who is sometimes alone and represents the Genius of the Senate, at other times is accompanied by the Emperor in the attitude of holding up a globe with him, the symbol of his assistance in supporting the burden of government. He is thus represented on a very rare bronze of Nerva, reproduced upon a unique silver medallion of Trajan (PROVIDENTIA SENATVS). On other coins the type suggests either the Concordia of the Senate with the Emperor or the piety of the Augustus, but always upon coins of extreme rarity.

III

THE PEOPLE.

GENIVS (or GENIVM) P R — GENIO POPVLI ROMANI.

The people is never represented except in an indirect or reflected manner upon the Imperial coinage. Its only representation is the Personification of its Genius, a male figure, nude, with patera and cornucopia, a modius upon the head, often in the act of pouring from the patera upon an altar. This personification, which was very rare at the beginning of the Empire, became extremely common under the four Emperors.

In a secondary subordinate line, the people is commemorated on several coins of Liberalitas, upon others of Games, or upon those which relate to public benefactions, as for example, upon those of Vitellius and Vespasian with the legend TVTELA AVGVSTI, of Trajan with ALIM. ITALIAE and similar coins, upon which the people is represented by some citizens or children.

The name of the Roman people is recorded abundantly upon all the coins which bear the legend SPQR and on many others which have types referring to the Emperor, to the Imperial family or to other personifications, bearing the legends CONCORDIA P R, FORTVNA P R, FELICITAS POP ROM or also GAVDIA GLORIA or VICTORIA ROMANORVM.

IV

THE ARMY.

COHORS PRAETORIANA — CONCORDIA or FIDES MILITVM, COHORTIVM PRAETORIANORVM, &c. — DISCIPLINA AVG — EXERCITVS BRITANNICVS, CAPPADOCICVS, DACICVS, GERMANICVS, HISPANICVS, ILLIRICIANVS, MAVRETANICVS, NORICVS, PARTHICVS, PERSICVS, RAETICVS — LEG PRI, II, III, IV, &c., ADIVTRIX, AVGVSTA, CLAVDIA, CLASSICA, FLAVIA, FRETENSIS, GEMINA, ITALICA, LYRICA, MACEDONICA, MACRIANA, MINERVINA, PARTHICA, PRIMIGENIA, SIRC (Carausius) TRAIANA, VLPIA, VICTRIX.

To this category are assigned principally the legionary coins of M. Antonius, Clodius Macrus, Albinus, Septimius Severus, Gallienus Carausius, and those of the cohorts of M. Antonius. These coins, generally bear as type the eagle between two military ensigns. But they often, especially in the case of Gallienus, present the special symbol of each legion : Mars, Minerva, Neptune, Victoria, the Bull, the Eagle, Lion, Centaur, Stork, Wolf, Capricorn, Pegasus, Wild Boar and so on.

Then follow the other much more numerous coins bearing the legend CONCORDIA or FIDES MILITVM or EXERCITVS which have their place among the types of the Allegorical Personifications.

A very beautiful series of coins of Hadrian commemorates all the armies of the Empire (EXERCITVS BRITANNICVS, SYRIACVS, &c.); the Emperor afoot or on horseback, who, to express it in modern terms, is reviewing the various armies, and this series can figure as well in this class as in that which regards the person of the Emperor.

The most complete series is that of Hadrian; but similar coins were struck also by others Emperors.

To this list may also be added those we have described already in the *Fasti Imperiali* with the legend ADLOCVTIO, and the others with the same scene of the *Adlocutio*, accompanied by the legend FIDES MILITVM (Commodus, Septimus Severus).

Finally we must add to this list those bearing a simple military emblem, one or more ensigns, a cuirass, one or two shields, a trophy, a gate of the camp, an intrenched camp, &c., &c.

V

PROVINCES, CITIES AND RIVERS.

AEGYPTOS — AFRICA — ALEXANDRIA — ARABIA — ARMENIA — ASIA — BRITANNIA — CAPPADOCIA — CONSTANTINOPOLIS — DACIA — DANIBIVS — FRANCIA — GALLIA — GERMANIA — HISPANIA — INVICTA ROMA — FELIX CARTHAGO — ITALIA — IVDAEA — MAVRETANIA — NILVS — PANNONIA — PHOENICE — SARMATIA — SCYTHIA — SICILIA — SYRIA — THRACIA — TIBERIS.

The Provinces and Cities of the Empire are commemorated on the coinage not only on occasions of the Imperial journeys or conquests, but are also figured on their own account. Augustus commemorated Hispania, Clodius Macrus Sicilia, Galba Hispania and Gallia, Vitellius Hispania, Trajanus Arabia and Dacia, Ælius Pannonia and Hispania, &c., &c., Hadrian and Antoninus many cities, provinces and rivers, and several provinces appear also later.

The Provinces are represented by a woman standing or seated and accompanied by some emblem which distinguishes her. Mauretania for example is in short dress with two darts, and holds a horse by the rein; Sicily bears on her head the triquetra, a crown and ears of corn are in her hand; Africa has the head ornamented with the elephant's trunk, places his right hand on a lion, the left on a chest of ears of corn; Germania is armed with lance and shield;

Syria bears a crown and cornucopia and has the river Orontes at her feet.

Italia turreted is furnished with sceptre and seated majestically upon a starry globe.

There belongs also to the Provinces the series of coins already seen in the Fasti Imperiali with the Emperor accompanied by the legend RESTITVTOR or RESTITVTORI.

Several rivers are represented upon the Imperial coinage. For the most part, it is indisputable that they are represented like the Provinces on their own account and, it might be said, geographically, but they may sometimes be considered as personifications of deity, as is said in its place in regard to the Nile in the time of Julian. Rivers are generally represented by a nude figure, lying down, and their emblems are the bulrush, crab, scorpion or hippopotamus, and the overturned urn from which water flows.

To this geographical list may be added the small series o coins commemorating the minerals, METALLI VLPIANI or VLPIANI DELM or VLPIANI PANN or METALLI PANNONICI of Trajan, AELIANA PINCENSIA, METAL AVRELIANVS, METAL NOR of Hadrian.

VI

PUBLIC EVENTS.

Public events of the Empire, victories, conquests, assignations of princes to foreign regions, internal events referring to Italy or the city of Rome, administrative innovations, institutions, games, extraordinary occurrences, all leave their trace upon the Imperial coinage.

Already the coins of Augustus point to the conquest of Egypt and Armenia (AEGYPTO CAPTA, ARMENIA DEVICTA), those of Nero Drusus to the German Victories (DE GERMANIS), those of Claudius to the Britannic conquests (DE BRITANNIS), those of Titus and Vespasian to the conquest of Judea (IVDAEA CAPTA, IVDAEA DEVICTA), those of Trajan to the conquests of Dacia (DACIA CAPTA), of Arabia (ARAB ADQVISIT), of Armenia and Mesopotamia (ARMENIA ET MESOPOTAMIA IN POTESTATEM PR REDACTAE) of Marcus Aurelius, Lucius Verus and Commodus to the victories obtained in Germany (DE GERMANIS or GERMANIA SVBACTA) or in Sarmatia (DE SARMATIS) and in continuation we ought to repeat here in great part the sketch already given in the second part of this work under the title Victoria.

The types not to be found quoted there are the assignations of the reign of Trajan (REGNA ADSIGNATA), the episode of the king of the Parthians (REX PARTHVS), the names of foreign kings of Antoninus Pius (REX ARMENIS and REX QVADIS DATVS) and so on.

Passing to internal events; Galba records the remission of taxes (XXXX REMISSA), Nerva, all the innovations made in his brief but provident government, the lightening of the tax upon the Hebrews (FISCI IVDAICI CALVMNIA SVBLATA) in which Iudea is represented by a palm-tree; the regulation of provisions to the Roman populace (PLEBEI VRBANAE FRVMENTO CONSTITVTO) symbolized by a modius filled with ears of corn, the condonation of the heavy imposition for the Imperial post which burdened all Italy (VEHICVLATIONE ITALIAE REMISSA) represented by two mules grazing.

Septimius Severus and Julia Domna record the remission to the Carthaginians of the impost for the acqueduct (INDVLGENTIA AVGG IN CARTHAGO) symbolized by the goddess of Carthage on a lion running or INDVLGENTIA AVGG IN ITALIAM of Severus and of Caracalla symbolized by Italia.

And other similar types may figure as belonging to the series having regard to the person of the Emperors.

VII

PRAYERS FOR THE EMPEROR.

VOTA OPTATA ROM FEL. — VOTA SUSCEPTA, SOLVTA — VOT V, VOT X &c. — VOT V MVLT X, VOT X MVLT XX &c. VOT V ET X, X ET XX &c. — VOTA AVG — VOTA CAES, VOTA DECENNALIA, VIGENNALIA &c. — VOTA ORBIS, PVBLICA, FELICIA, ROMANORVM, &c., &c.

The coins which refer to prayers for the Emperor are very numerous. Generally the legend is in a laurel wreath; but other types are often found; sometimes it is a Victory who inscribes the prayers on a shield held upon her knee, or leaning against a palm tree or a cippus; or it is held by a small Genius. Sometimes two Victories hold the votive shield, or the inscription accompanies the figure of the Emperor sacrificing upon a tripod, or it is a complete scene of sacrifice before a temple.

All these types are related to those referring to the person of the Emperor. And to them also may belong those referring to the prayers for the health of the Emperor or to thanksgivings for restoration to health. IOVI VOT SVSC PRO SA CAES AVG SPQR — VOT P SVSC PRO SAL ET RED IOM SACR — PRO VALETVDINE CAESARIS S P Q R (Augustus) OB CONSERVATIONEM SALVTIS (Gallienus), &c.

VIII

GAMES.

The organization of Games among the Romans was of great importance and became a truly public event. Thus we see recorded those established or set in motion by several Emperors, as Augustus (LVDI SAECVL), Nero (CERTAMEN QVINQ ROM CON), Domitian (LVD SAEC FEC), Hadrian (P CIR CON), Antoninus Pius (LVD DEC), Caracalla (LVD SAEC FEC).

Sometimes the inscription is upon a cippus, sometimes the Emperor at sacrifice is in the act of invoking the divinity on the opening of the games, or in the act of celebrating the inauguration or of taking part in the games themselves. Sometimes the game is symbolized by a gaming table.

As a record of solemnities celebrated at Rome, besides the dionysiac Medallions of Hadrian, of Antoninus Pius and M. Aurelius struck on the occasion of the great circus games, those of Septimius Severus and his sons on the occasion of the secular feasts (SAECVLARIA SACRA), that with the Colossus of Alexander and of Gordianus (MVNIFICENTIA GORDIANI AVG) we may quote the large series of coins in all metals issued by Philip the Elder, on the occasion of the solemn festivals to celebrate the millenium of Rome, with the three legends SAECVLVM NOVVM, MILLIARIVM SAECVLVM and SAECVLARES AVGG representing the two Philips seated, the temple of Rome, a commemorative cippus, or a series of animals symbolizing the games of the circus.

IX

MONUMENTS.

The first examples of the reproduction of public monuments upon the coinage occur in the time of the Republic, and I will quote the Basilica Æmilia upon the denarii of Emilius Lepidus, the Villa Publica upon those of T. Didius, the temple of Neptune upon the Aureus of Domitius Ænobarbus.

Such reproductions increase with the Empire, and to give only a few examples, Augustus commemorates upon his coins the Altar of Peace and the Altar of the Lion, the Temple of Jupiter Tonans, of Jupiter Olympus and of Mars Ultor, the Triumphal Arch after the Parthian Victory, the Aqueduct; Nero the Triumphal Arch, the Golden House, the Gate of Ostia, the Temple of Janus; Titus the

Colossus; Trajan the Basilica Ulpia, the Trajan Forum, the Trajan Aqueduct Way and Column, the Trajan Gate; Antoninus Pius the Temple of Augustus; Livia the Column of Antonina; Caracalla the Circus and the Baths; Alexander and Gordianus the Circus; Volusianus the Temple of the martial Juno; a complete enumeration would be too long.

PROTAT BROTHERS, PRINTERS, MACON (FRANCE)

THE PORTRAIT COIN-TYPES
OF IMPERIAL ROME
EMPERORS - CAESARS - FAMILIES
COMMEMORATIVES & MEDALS

THE PORTRAIT COIN-TYPES OF IMPERIAL ROME

EMPERORS - CAESARS - FAMILIES COMMEMORATIVES & MEDALS

By

GEORGE ELMER

ARES PUBLISHERS INC.
CHICAGO MCMLXXVIII

+ = Coin Exists

+• = Coin is lost and known only from impressions, drawings or descriptions.

• = Coin is not known to exist

Regnal Dates		Gold: Quaternio	Gold: Aureus	Gold: Half Aureus	Silver: Denarius	Silver: Quinarius	Medallion in Bronze or Brass	Brass: Sestertius	Brass: Dupondius	Brass: As	Brass: Semis	Brass: Quadrans	Bronze: As	Bronze: Semis	Bronze: Small Bronze	Bronze: Half Small Bronze
16 Jan. 27 B.C. 19 Aug. 14. A.D.	**Augustus,** Imperator Caesar Augustus	+	+	+	+	+	+	+	+	•	•	•	+	•	+	•
	Augustus and Divus Julius (Julius Caesar, great-uncle and adopted father)	•	+	•	+	•	•	•	•	•	•	•	•	•	•	•
	and Marcus Agrippa (son-in-law)	•	+	•	+	•	•	•	•	•	•	•	•	•	•	•
	and Julia (daughter), Caius and Lucius (grandsons, later adopted)	•	•	•	+	•	•	•	•	•	•	•	•	•	•	•
	and Julia	•	•	•	+	•	•	•	•	•	•	•	•	•	•	•
	and Caius Caesar (grandson, adopted son and heir apparent)	•	+	•	+	•	•	•	•	•	•	•	•	•	•	•
	and Caius and Lucius Caesars (grandsons, adopted sons and heirs apparent)	+	+	•	+	•	•	•	•	•	•	•	•	•	•	•
	and Tiberius Caesar (heir apparent, adopted and step-son)	•	+	•	+	•	•	•	•	•	•	•	•	•	•	•
	Tiberius Caesar	•	•	•	•	•	•	•	•	•	•	•	+	•	•	•
19 Aug. 14 A.D. 16 March 37	**Tiberius,** Tiberius Caesar	•	+	+	+	•	•	+	+	•	•	•	+	•	•	•
	Divus Augustus (adopted father)	•	•	•	•	•	•	•	+	•	•	•	+	•	•	•
	and Divus Augustus	•	+	•	•	•	•	+	•	•	•	•	•	•	•	•
	and Julia (Livia, his mother, widow of Augustus)	•	•	•	•	•	•	+	+	•	•	•	•	•	•	•
	Drusus Caesar (Drusus the younger, son and heir apparent)	•	•	•	•	•	•	+	+	•	•	•	+	•	•	•
	Marcus Agrippa (father-in-law)	•	•	•	•	•	•	•	•	•	•	•	+	•	•	•
18 March 37- 24 Jan. 41	**Caius,** Caius Caesar Germanicus (**Caligula**)	•	+	+	+	•	•	+	•	•	•	•	+	•	+	•
	Divus Augustus (great-grandfather)	•	•	•	•	•	•	•	+	•	•	•	•	•	•	•
	Germanicus Caesar (father)	•	•	•	•	•	•	•	+	•	•	•	•	•	•	•
	Agrippina the elder (mother)	•	•	•	•	•	•	+	•	•	•	•	•	•	•	•
	Caius and Divus Augustus	•	+	•	+	•	•	+	•	•	•	•	•	•	•	•
	and Germanicus Caesar	•	+	•	+	•	•	•	•	•	•	•	+	•	•	•
	and Agrippina the elder	•	+	•	+	•	•	•	•	•	•	•	•	•	•	•
	and Nero Caesar with Drusus Caesar (brothers)	•	•	•	•	•	•	•	+	•	•	•	•	•	•	•
	and Agrippina the younger, Drusilla and Julia (sisters)	•	•	•	•	•	•	+	•	•	•	•	•	•	•	•
25 Jan. 41- 13 Oct. 54	**Claudius,** Tiberius Claudius Caesar Germanicus	•	+	+	+	•	•	+	+	•	•	•	+	•	+	•
	Divus Augustus (great-uncle) and Diva Augusta (Livia, grandmother)	•	•	•	•	•	•	•	+	•	•	•	•	•	•	•
	Nero Claudius Drusus Germanicus (Drusus the Elder, father)	•	+	•	+	•	•	•	•	•	•	•	•	•	•	•
	Antonia (mother)	•	+	•	+	•	•	•	•	•	•	•	•	•	•	•
	and Drusus the elder	•	•	•	•	•	•	+	•	•	•	•	•	•	•	•
	and Antonia	•	•	•	•	•	•	•	+	•	•	•	•	•	•	•
	and Germanicus Caesar (brother)	•	•	•	•	•	•	+	•	•	•	•	+	•	•	•
	and Agrippina the elder (sister-in-law)	•	•	•	•	•	•	+	•	•	•	•	•	•	•	•
	Tiberius Claudius Caesar Britannicus (son)	•	•	•	•	•	•	+	•	•	•	•	•	•	•	•
	and Agrippina the younger (niece and consort)	•	+	•	+	•	•	•	•	•	•	•	•	•	•	•
	Nero Claudius Caesar Drusus Germanicus (grand-nephew, adopted son and heir apparent)	•	+	•	+	•	•	•	•	•	•	•	•	•	•	•
	and Nero	•	+	•	+	•	•	•	•	•	•	•	•	•	•	•
	Agrippina the younger and Nero	•	•	•	+	•	•	•	•	•	•	•	•	•	•	•
13 Oct. 54- 9 June 68	**Nero,** Nero Claudius Caesar Germanicus	•	+	+	+	•	•	+	+	+	+	+	+	+	+	+
	Divus Claudius (adopted father and great-uncle)	•	+	•	+	•	•	•	•	•	•	•	•	•	•	•
	Nero and Agrippina the younger (mother)	•	+	•	+	•	•	•	•	•	•	•	•	•	•	•

+ = Coin Exists

+. = Coin is lost and known only from impressions, drawings or descriptions.

• = Coin is not known to exist

Regnal dates		Gold		Silver		Brass		Bronze	
		Aureus	Half Aureus	Denarius	Quinarius	Sestertius	Dupondius	As	Quadrans
March 68-end of 70	**Civil War** coinage under Nero, Galba Otho, Vitellius and Vespasian without name of issuing authority	+	.	+	.	.	.	.	.
	Augustus, i.e. Divus Augustus	+	.	+	.	.	.	.	.
	Augustus and Divus Julius	.	.	+	.	.	.	.	.
	Clodius Macer, governor in Africa	.	.	+	.	.	.	.	.
	Servius Galba, governor in Spain	+	.	+	.	.	.	.	.
	Galba and Diva Augusta (Livia, consort of Augustus)	.	.	+	.	.	.	.	.
	Aulus Vitellius, governor in Germania	+	.	+	.	.	.	+	.
	Aulus Vitellius and his children	+	.	+	.	.	.	.	.
	Aulus Vitellius and Lucius Vitellius (father)	+	.	+	.	.	.	.	.
July 68-15 Jan. 69	**Galba,** Servius Sulpicius Galba	+	.	+	.	+	+	+	.
	Galba and Diva Augusta (Livia, consort of Augusta)	+	.	+	.	+	+	+	.
15 Jan.-17 April 69	**Otho,** Marcus Otho	+	.	+	.	.	.	.	.
18 July-20 Dec. 69	**Vitellius,** Aulus Vitellius	+	.	+	.	+	+	+	.
	Vitellius and his children	+	.	+	.	.	.	.	.
	and Lucius Vitellius (father)	+	.	+	.	+	.	.	.
1 July 69-23 June 79	**Vespasianus,** Flavius Vespasianus	+	+	+	+	+	+	+	+
	Servius Sulpicius Galba	+	.	+	+	+	+	+	.
	Titus Vespasianus (son and heir apparent)	+	+	+	+	+	+	+	.
	Domitianus (son and heir apparent)	+	+	+	+	+	+	+	.
	Vespasianus, Titus and Domitianus	+	.	+	.	+	.	+	.
	Vespasianus and Titus	+	.	.	.	.	.	.	.
	Titus and Domitianus	.	.	.	.	+	.	.	.
23 June 79-13 Sept. 81	**Titus,** Titus Vespasianus	+	.	+	+	+	+	+	+
	Divus Vespasianus (father)	+	.	+	+	+	+	+	.
	Titus and Divus Vespasianus	+	.	.	.	+	.	.	.
	and Domitilla (mother)	.	.	.	.	+	.	.	.
	Julia (daughter)	.	.	+	.	.	+	.	.
	Domitianus (brother and heir apparent)	+	.	+	+	+	+	+	.
	Restitution issues with the name of Titus by:								
	Tiberius	.	.	.	.	+	+	+	.
	Divus Augustus	.	.	.	.	+	+	+	.
	Drusus Caesar (Drusus the younger)	.	.	.	.	.	.	+	.
	Marcus Agrippa	.	.	.	.	.	.	+	.
	Claudius	.	.	.	.	+	+	+	.
	Nero Claudius Drusus Germanicus (Drusus the elder)	.	.	.	.	+	.	.	.
	Germanicus Caesar	.	.	.	.	.	.	+	.
	Agrippina the elder	.	.	.	.	+	.	.	.

+ = Coin Exists

+• = Coin is lost and known only from impressions, drawings or descriptions.

• = Coin is not known to exist

Regnal dates		Gold				Silver		Brass				Bronze	
		Octonio	Quaternio	Aureus	Half Aureus	Denarius	Quinarius	Sestertius	Dupondius	Semis	Triens	As	Quadrans
13 Sept. 81 18 Sept. 96	**Domitianus**	+•	+•	+	+	+	+	+	+	+	•	+	+
	Divus Vespasianus and Diva Domitilla (parents)	•	•	+	•	•	•	•	•	•	•	•	•
	Diva Domitilla (mother)	•	•	•	•	+	•	•	•	•	•	•	•
	Divus Titus Vespasianus (brother)	•	•	•	•	•	•	+	•	•	•	•	•
	Domitianus and Divus Titus Vespasianus	•	•	•	•	•	•	+	•	•	•	•	•
	Divus Titus and Julia (niece, daughter of Titus)	•	•	+	•	•	•	•	•	•	•	•	•
	Julia	•	•	+	•	•	•	•	•	•	•	•	•
	Domitianus and Diva Julia	•	•	•	•	•	•	+	•	•	•	•	•
	Domitianus and Domitia (consort)	•	•	+	•	•	•	•	•	•	•	•	•
	Domitia	•	•	+	•	+	•	+	+	•	•	•	•
	Domitia and Divus Caesar (son)	•	•	+	•	+	•	•	•	•	•	•	•
	Restitution issues with the name of Domitianus by:												
	Tiberius												
	Divus Augustus	•	•	•	•	•	•	•	•	•	•	+	•
	Drusus Caesar (= Drusus the younger)	•	•	•	•	•	•	•	•	•	•	+	•
	Marcus Agrippa	•	•	•	•	•	•	•	•	•	•	+	•
	Claudius	•	•	•	•	•	•	•	•	•	•	+	•
	Germanicus Caesar	•	•	•	•	•	•	•	•	•	•	+	•
18 Sept. 96- 25 Jan. 98	**Nerva**	•	•	+	+	+	+	+	+	+	•	+	+
	Restitution issues with Nerva's name for:												
	Divus Augustus	•	•	•	•	+	•	+	+	•	•	+	•
27 Jan. 98- 9 Aug. 117	**Traianus**, Nerva Traianus	+•	+•	+	+	+	+	+	+	+	•	+	•
	Traianus and Divus Traianus pater (father)	•	•	+	•	+	•	•	•	•	•	•	•
	Traianus, Divus Nerva (adopted father) and Divus Traianus pater	•	•	+	•	•	•	•	•	•	•	•	•
	Plotina (consort)	•	•	+	+	+	•	+	•	•	•	•	•
	Marciana (sister), and her daughter, Matidia (niece)	•	•	+	•	+	•	•	•	•	•	•	•
	Diva Marciana	•	•	+	+	+	•	+	•	•	•	•	•
	Matidia	•	•	+	•	+	•	+	•	•	•	•	•
	Traianus and Hadrianus Traianus (nephew, adopted son and heir apparent)	•	•	+•	•	•	•	•	•	•	•	•	•
	Restitution issues with the name of Traianus for:												
	The Roman Republic (with and without names of moneyers)	•	•	•	•	•	•	•	•	•	•	•	•
	Caesar Augustus or Divus Augustus	•	•	•	•	•	•	•	•	•	•	•	•
	Augustus and Marcus Agrippa	•	•		•	+	•	•	•	•	•	•	•
	Tiberius Caesar	•	•	+	•	•	•	•	•	•	•	•	•
	Tiberius Claudius Caesar or Divus Claudius Galba	•	•	+	•	•	•	•	•	•	•	•	•
	Galba	•	•	+	•	•	•	•	•	•	•	•	•
	Civil War period (68-70)	•	•	+	•	•	•	•	•	•	•	•	•
	Vespasianus or Divus Vespasianus	•	•	•	•	•	•	•	•	•	•	•	•
	Titus Vespasianus or Divus Titus	•	•	+	•	•	•	•	•	•	•	•	•
	Divus Nerva	•	•	+	•	•	•	•	•	•	•	•	•

Regnal dates	+ = Coin Exists +• = Coin is lost and known only from impressions, drawings or descriptions. • = Coin is not known to exist	Gold			Silver		Medallion in Brass	Brass			Bronze	
		Octonio	Aureus	Half Aureus	Denarius	Quinarius		Sestertius	Dupondius	Semis	As	Quadrans
11 Aug. 117- 10 July 138	**Hadrianus,** Traianus Hadrianus	+•	+	+	+	+	+	+	+	+	+	+
	Divus Traianus (uncle and adopted father)	•	+	•	•	•	•	•	•	•	•	•
	Hadrianus and Divus Traianus	•	+	•	•	•	•	+	•	•	•	•
	Plotina (adopted mother)	•	+	+	•	•	•	•	•	•	•	•
	Divus Traianus and Plotina or Diva Plotina (adopted parents)	•	+	•	•	•	•	•	•	•	•	•
	and Divus Traianus with Diva Plotina	•	+	•	•	•	•	•	•	•	•	•
	and Plotina	•	+	•	•	•	•	•	•	•	•	•
	and Diva Matidia (mother-in-law)	•	•	•	•	•	+	•	•	•	•	•
	Plotina and Matidia	•	+	•	•	•	•	•	•	•	•	•
	Diva Matidia	•	+	•	+	•	•	•	•	•	•	•
	Sabina or Diva Sabina (consort)	•	+	+	+	•	+	+	+	•	+	•
	Lucius Aelius (adopted son and heir apparent)	•	+	+	+	•	+	+	+	•	+	•
	Titus Aelius Antoninus (adopted son and heir apparent)	•	+	+	+	•	+	+	+	•	+	•
	Restitution issues with Hadrian's name for:											
	Divus Traianus	•	•	•	+	•	•	•	•	•	•	•
10 July 138- 7 March 161	**Antoninus (I)**, Titus Aelius Hadrianus Antoninus, called **Pius**	•	+	+	+	+	+	+	+	+	+	•
	Divus Hadrianus (adopted father)	•	+	•	+	•	•	+	•	•	•	•
	Faustina the elder or Diva Faustina (consort)	•	+	+	+	•	+	+	+	•	+	•
	Aurelius (Marcus Aurelius, nephew, adopted son and heir apparent)	•	+	+	+	•	+	+	+	•	+	•
	Antoninus and Aurelius	•	+	•	+	•	+	+	+	•	+	•
	Faustina the younger (daughter, consort of Marcus Aurelius)	•	+	+	+	•	+	+	+	•	+	•
7 March 161- 17 March 180	**Antoninus (II)**, Marcus Aurelius Antoninus, called **Marcus Aurelius**	•	+	+	+	+	+	+	+	•	+	•
	Faustina the younger or Diva Faustina (consort)	•	+	+	+	•	+	+	+	•	+	•
	Divus Verus (son-in-law)	•	•	•	+	•	•	+	•	•	•	•
	Lucius Aurelius Commodus (son and heir apparent)	•	+	•	+	•	+	+	+	•	+	•
	Antoninus and Commodus	•	•	•	+	•	+	•	•	•	•	•
	Commodus and Annius Verus (sons and heirs apparent)	•	•	•	•	•	+	•	•	•	•	•
March 161- Feb. 169	**Verus,** Lucius Aurelius Verus	+•	+	+	+	+	+	+	+	•	+	•
	Lucilla (consort, daughter of Marcus Aurelius)	•	+	•	+	•	+	+	+	•	+	•
161—169	**Antoninus (II)**, and **Verus**	•	•	•	•	•	+	•	•	•	•	•
	Divus Antoninus (adopted father)	•	+	•	+	•	+	+	•	•	+	•
	Restitution issues in the name of Antoninus and Verus for:											
	Antonius augur III vir rei publicae constituendae	•	•	•	+	•	•	•	•	•	•	•
177-180	**Antoninus (II)**, Marcus Aurelius Antoninus and **Commodus,** Lucius Aurelius Commodus	•	•	•	•	•	+	•	•	•	•	•

+ = Coin Exists

+• = Coin is lost and known only from impressions, drawings or descriptions.

• = Coin is not known to exist

Regnal dates		Gold: Multiple Aurei	Gold: Binio	Gold: Aureus	Gold: Half Aureus	Silver: Medallion	Silver: Antoninianus	Silver: Denarius	Silver: Quinarius	Medallion in Brass or Bronze	Brass: Sestertius	Brass: Dupondius	Bronze: As
Early Summer 177-31 Dec. 192	**Commodus,** Lucius Marcus Aelius Aurelius Commodus Antoninus	+•	•	+	+	•	•	+	+	+	+	+	+
	Divus Marcus Antoninus (father)	•	•	+	•	•	•	+	•	•	+	•	+
	Crispina (consort)	•	•	+	•	•	•	+	•	+	+	+	+
	Commodus and Crispina	•	•	•	•	•	•	•	•	+	•	•	•
1 Jan.—28 March 193	**Pertinax,** Publius Helvius Pertinax	•	•	+	•	•	•	+	•	•	+	+	+
28 March—1 June 193	**Didius Julianus,** Marcus Didius Severus Julianus	•	•	+	•	•	•	+	•	•	+	+	•
	Manlia Scantilla (consort)	•	•	+	•	•	•	+	•	•	+	+	•
	Didia Clara (daughter)	•	•	+	•	•	•	+	•	•	+	+	•
13 April 193-4 Feb. 211	**Severus,** Lucius Septimius Severus Pertinax	+•	•	+	+	•	•	+	+	+	+	+	+
	Divus Pertinax (pretended adopted father)	•	•	+	•	•	•	+	•	•	+	•	•
	Decimus Clodius Septimius Albinus (adopted son and heir apparent)	•	•	+	+	•	•	+	•	+	+	+	+
	Julia Domna (consort)	+•	•	+	+	•	•	+	+	+	+	+	+
	Marcus Aurelius Antoninus (Caracalla, son and heir apparent)	•	•	+	•	•	•	+	•	+	+	•	+
	Lucius Publius Septimius Geta (son and heir apparent)	+•	•	+	•	•	•	+	+	+	+	•	+
April 193—Oct. 194	**Niger,** Caius Pescennius Niger Justus, in Syria	•	•	+	•	•	•	+	•	•	•	•	•
Fall 196-19 Feb. 197	**Albinus,** Decimus Clodius Septimius Albinus, in the West	•	•	+	•	•	•	+	•	•	•	•	•
198-209	**Severus** and **Antoninus** (III-Caracalla)	•	•	+	•	•	•	+	•	•	•	•	•
	Severus and Julia (consort)	•	•	+	•	•	•	+	•	•	•	•	•
	Severus and Geta (son and heir apparent)	•	•	+	•	•	•	+	•	•	•	•	•
	Severus, Antoninus, Julia and Geta	•	•	+	•	•	•	+	•	•	•	•	•
	Severus, Antoninus and Julia	•	•	+	•	•	•	•	•	•	•	•	•
	Severus, Antoninus and Geta	•	•	+	•	•	•	+	•	•	•	•	•
	Severus Julia and Geta	•	•	+	•	•	•	+	•	•	•	•	•
	Antoninus and Julia (mother)	•	•	+	•	•	•	+	•	•	•	•	•
	Antoninus and Geta (brother)	•	•	+	•	•	•	+	•	•	•	•	•
	Antoninus, Julia and Geta	•	•	+	•	•	•	+	•	•	•	•	•
	Julia and Geta	•	•	+	•	•	•	+	•	•	•	•	•
Early Jan. 198-8 April 217	**Antoninus** (III), Marcus Aurelius Antoninus, Called **Caracalla**	+•	+	+	+	+	+	+	+	+	+	•	•
	Julia (mother)	•	+	+	+	•	+	+	+	•	+	+	•
	Plautilla (consort)	•	•	+	•	•	•	+	+	•	+	+	•
	Antoninus and Plautilla	•	•	+	•	•	•	•	•	•	•	•	•
211-212	**Antoninus** (III) and **Geta** for:												
	Divus Severus (father)	•	•	+	•	•	•	•	•	•	•	•	•
	Julia (mother)	•	•	+	•	•	•	+	•	•	+	•	•

+ = Coin Exists

+• = Coin is lost and known only from impressions, drawings or descriptions.

• = Coin is not known to exist

Regnal dates		Gold					Silver					Brass		Bronze
		Multiple Aurei	Octonio	Binio	Aureus	Half Aureus	Medallion	Antoninianus	Denarius	Quinarius	Medallion in Bronze or Brass	Sestertius	Dupondius	As
Sept. or Oct. 209-26 Feb. 212	**Geta,** Publius Septimius Geta	+•	•	•	+	•	•	•	+	•	•	+	+	+
11 April 217-8 June 218	**Macrinus,** Marcus Opelius Severus Macrinus	•	•	•	+	+	•	+	+	+	•	+	+	+
	Marcus Opelius Antoninus Diadumenianus (son and heir apparent)	•	•	•	+	+	•	+	+	+	•	+	+	+
16 May 218-11 March 222	**Antoninus** (IV), Marcus Aurelius Antoninus, called **Elagabalus**	+•	•	+	+	+	+	+	+	+	+	+	+	+
	Julia Maesa (grandmother)	+•	•	•	+	•	•	+	+	+	•	+	+	+
	Julia Soaemias (mother)	+•	•	•	+	•	•	•	+	+	•	+	+	+
	Marcus Aurelius Alexander (cousin and heir apparent)	•	•	•	•	•	•	•	+	•	•	+	•	+
	Divus Antoninus Magnus (Caracalla, uncle)	•	•	•	•	•	•	•	+	•	•	+	•	•
	Diva Julia (Caracalla's mother, great-aunt)	•	•	•	•	•	•	•	+	•	+	+	•	•
	Julia Paula (consort)	+•	•	•	+	•	•	•	+	+	•	+	+	+
	Julia Aquilia Severa (consort)	+•	•	•	•	•	•	•	+	+	•	+	+	+
	Antoninus and Severa	•	•	•	•	•	•	•	•	•	+	•	•	•
	Annia Faustina (consort)	•	•	•	•	•	•	•	+	•	•	+	•	•
11 March 222-19 March 235	**Alexander,** Marcus Aurelius Severus Alexander	+•	+	+	+	+	+	•	+	+	+	+	+	+
	Julia Maesa, or Diva Maesa (grandmother)	•	•	•	+	•	•	•	+	+	•	+	+	+
	Julia Mamias or Julia Mamaea (mother)	+•	•	•	+	+	•	•	+	+	+	+	+	+
	Alexander and Mamaea	+•	•	•	•	•	+	•	•	•	+	•	•	•
	Sallustia Barbia Orbiana (consort)	•	•	•	+	•	•	•	+	+	+	+	•	+
	Alexander and Orbiana	•	•	•	•	•	•	•	•	•	+	•	•	•
	Alexander, Mamaea and Orbiana	+•	•	•	•	•	•	•	•	•	•	•	•	•
Before 19 March 235-May 238	**Maximinus,** called Thrax	•	•	•	+	+	+	•	+	+	+	+	+	+
	Diva Paulina (consort)	•	•	•	•	•	•	•	+	•	•	+	•	•
	Caius Julius Verus Maximus (son and heir apparent)	•	•	•	+	•	•	•	+	+	•	+	+	+
	Maximinus and Maximus	•	•	•	•	•	•	•	•	•	+	•	•	•
Early to late March, 238	**Gordianus** (I), Marcus Antonius Gordianus Africanus	•	•	•	+	•	•	•	+	•	•	+	•	•
	Gordianus (II), Marcus Antonius Gordianus Africanus, son of Gordianus I	•	•	•	+	•	•	•	+	•	•	+	•	•
Early April Mid-July 238	**Pupienus,** Marcus Clodius Pupienus Maximus	•	•	•	+	•	•	+	+	•	+	+	+	+
	Balbinus, Decimus Caelius Balbinus	•	•	•	+	•	•	+	+	•	+	+	+	+
	Pupienus and **Balbinus** for their heir apparent: Marcus Antonius Gordianus, grandson of Gordian I	•	•	•	•	•	•	•	+	•	•	+	•	+

+ = Coin Exists

+• = Coin is lost and known only from impressions, drawings or descriptions.

• = Coin is not known to exist

Regnal dates		Gold: Multiple Aurei	Gold: Quaternio	Gold: Binio	Gold: Aureus	Gold: Half Aureus	Silver: Medallion	Silver: Antoninianus	Silver: Denarius	Silver: Quinarius	Medallion in Bronze or Brass	Brass: Double Sestertius	Brass: Sestertius	Brass: Dupondius	Bronze: As	Bronze: Triens
Mid-July 238 Feb. 244	**Gordianus** (III), Marcus Antonius Gordianus, grandson of Gordian I	•	•	+	+	+	+	+	+	+	+	•	+	+	+	•
	Sabina Tranquillina (consort)	•	•	•	•	•	•	+	+	•	•	•	+	•	+	•
Feb. 244-Sept. or Oct. 249	**Philippus** the elder, Marcus Julius Philippus, called the Arab	•	+	•	+	+	+	+	+	+	+	•	+	+	+	•
	Marcia Otacilia Severa (consort)	•	•	•	+	•	•	+	+	+	+	•	+	+	+	•
	Marcus Julius Philippus the younger (son and heir apparent)	•	•	•	+	•	•	+	+	+	+	•	+	+	+	•
	Philippus the elder, Severa and Philippus the younger	+•	•	•	•	•	•	+	+	•	+	•	•	•	•	•
	and Severa	•	•	•	•	•	•	•	•	•	+	•	•	•	•	•
	and Philippus the younger	•	•	•	•	•	•	•	•	•	+	•	•	•	•	•
247-249	**Philippus** the elder and **Philippus the younger**	•	•	•	•	•	•	•	•	•	+	•	•	•	•	•
	Philippus the elder, Philippus the younger and Severa	•	•	•	•	•	•	+	•	•	+	•	•	•	•	•
July 247- Sept. or Oct. 249	**Philippus** the younger, Marcus Julius Phillippus	•	•	•	+	•	+	+	•	+	+	•	+	+	+	•
248	**Jotapianus,** Marcus Fulvius? Rufus? Jotapianus, in Syria	•	•	•	•	•	•	+	•	•	•	•	•	•	•	•
Early Summer 248	**Pacatianus,** Tiberius Claudius Marinus Pacatianus, in Moesia	•	•	•	•	•	•	+	•	•	•	•	•	•	•	•
248-254	**Uranius Antoninus,** Lucius Julius Sulpicius Uranius Antoninus, in Syria	•	•	•	+	•	•	•	•	•	•	•	•	•	•	•
Late Oct. 248- Late May 251	**Decius** the elder, Caius Messius Quintus Traianus Decius	•	•	•	+	+•	+	+	•	+	+	+	+	+	+	+
	Herennia Etruscilla (consort)	•	•	•	+	•	+	+	•	+	+	+	+	+	+	•
	Decius the elder and Etruscilla	•	•	•	•	•	•	•	•	•	•	•	+	•	•	•
	Quintus Herennius Etruscus Messius Decius the younger, son and heir apparent	+•	•	•	+	•	•	+	•	+	+	•	+	+	+	•
	Caius Valens Hostilianus Messius Quintus (son and heir apparent)	•	•	•	+	•	•	+	•	+	+	•	+	+	+	•
	Decius the elder, Etruscilla, Decius the younger and Quintus	•	•	•	•	•	•	+	•	•	+	•	•	•	•	•
	and Decius the younger with Quintus	•	•	•	•	•	•	+	•	•	+	•	•	•	•	•
Spring— late May 251	**Decius** the younger, Quintus Herennius Etruscus Messius Decius	•	•	•	+	•	•	+	•	•	•	•	•	•	•	•
Spring- Nov. 251	**Quintus,** Caius Valens Hostilianus Messius Quintus	•	•	•	+	•	•	+	•	•	•	•	+	•	+	•
June 251- Aug. 253	**Gallus,** Caius Vibius Trebonianus Gallus	•	•	+	+	•	+	•	•	+	+	+	+	+	+	•
251	**Gallus** and **Quintus** for their heir apparent: Caius Vibius Trebonianus, son of Gallus	•	•	•	+	•	•	•	•	•	•	•	+	•	+	•
Nov. 251- Aug. 253	**Volusianus,** Caius Vibius Afinius Gallus Vendumnianus Volusianus	+•	•	+	+	•	+	+	•	+	+	+	+	+	•	•
251-253	**Gallus** and **Volusianus**	•	•	•	•	•	•	•	•	•	+	•	•	•	•	•

+ = Coin Exists

+• = Coin is lost and known only from impressions, drawings or descriptions.

• . = Coin is not known to exist

Regnal dates		Gold: Multiple Aurei	Gold: Octonio	Gold: Quaternio	Gold: Binio	Gold: Aureus	Gold: Half Aureus	Silver (Bronze with Silver Wash): Medallion	Silver (Bronze with Silver Wash): Antoninianus	Silver (Bronze with Silver Wash): Denarius	Silver (Bronze with Silver Wash): Quinarius	Medallion in Bronze or Brass	Brass: Sestertius	Brass: Dupondius	Bronze: As
May-Oct. 253	**Aemilianus,** Marcus Aemilius Aemilianus	.	.	.	.	+	.	.	+	.	.	.	+	+	+
	Gaia Cornelia Supera (consort)	.	.	.	.	.	.	.	+	.	.	.	.	.	.
Sept. 253-258 or 259	**Valerianus** the elder, Publius Licinius Valerianus	+•	.	.	+	+	+	+	+	.	+	+	+	+	+
	Diva Mariniana (consort)	+•	.	.	.	+	.	.	+	.	+	.	+	+	+
253-259	**Valerianus** the elder and **Gallienus**	+•	.	+•	.	.	.	+	.	.	.	+	.	.	.
	Valerianus the elder, Gallienus, Salonina (consort of Gallienus) and Valerianus the younger (son of Gallienus, heir apparent)	+•	.	.	.	.	.	.	.	.	.	.	.	.	.
	Valerianus the elder and his grandson, Valerianus and the younger	.	.	.	.	.	.	.	.	.	.	+	.	.	.
	Galienus and his son Valerianus the younger	+•	.	.	.	.	.	.	.	.	.	.	.	.	.
	Publius Cornelius Licinius Valerianus the younger, (heir apparent)	.	.	.	.	+	+	.	+	.	+	.	+	.	+
	Consecration issues for:														
	Divus Augustus	.	.	.	.	.	.	.	+	.	.	.	.	.	.
	Divus Vespasianus	.	.	.	.	.	.	.	+	.	.	.	.	.	.
	Divus Titus	.	.	.	.	.	.	.	+	.	.	.	.	.	.
	Divus Nerva	.	.	.	.	.	.	.	+	.	.	.	.	.	.
	Divus Traianus	.	.	.	.	.	.	.	+	.	.	.	.	.	.
	Divus Hadrianus	.	.	.	.	.	.	.	+	.	.	.	.	.	.
	Divus Pius (Antoninus Pius)	.	.	.	.	.	.	.	+	.	.	.	.	.	.
	Divus Marcus or Marcus Antoninus (Marcus Aurelius)	.	.	.	.	.	.	.	+	.	.	.	.	.	.
	Divus Commodus	.	.	.	.	.	.	.	+	.	.	.	.	.	.
	Divus Severus	.	.	.	.	.	.	.	+	.	.	.	.	.	.
	Divus Alexander	.	.	.	.	.	.	.	+	.	.	.	.	.	.
Oct. 253-early March 268	**Gallienus,** Publius Licinius Gallienus	+•	+•	+	+	+	+	+	+	+	+	+	+	+	+
	Cornelia Salonina (consort)	+•	.	.	.	+	.	.	+	+	+	+	+	.	+
	Gallienus and Salonina	+•	+	.	+	+	.	.	.	.	.	.	.	.	.
	Divus Valerianus the younger (son)	.	.	.	.	+	.	.	+	.	.	.	+	.	.
	Publius Licinius Cornelius Saloninus Valerianus (son and heir apparent)	+•	.	.	+	+	.	+	+	.	+	+	+	.	+
	Gallienus and Marinianus (probable son)	.	+•	.	.	.	.	.	.	.	.	.	.	.	.
	and Deus Augustus	.	.	.	+	.	.	.	.	.	.	.	.	.	.
Late 259-early 260	**Saloninus Valerianus,** son of Gallienus, in Gaul	.	.	.	.	+	.	.	+	.	.	.	.	.	.
Late 259-mid 268	**Postumus,** Marcus Cassianus Latinius Postumus, in the West	+•	.	.	+	+	+	.	+	.	+	+	+	+	.
Sept. 261-June 262	**Macrianus,** Fulvis Macrianus, in the East	.	.	.	.	+	.	.	+	.	.	.	.	.	.
	Quietus, Fulvius Quietus, brother of Macrianus	+•	.	.	.	+	.	.	+	.	.	.	.	.	.
Ca. 262	**Regalianus,** Publius? Cornelius? Regalianus, in north Pannonia	.	.	.	.	.	.	.	+	.	.	.	.	.	.
	Sulpicia Dryantilla (consort)	.	.	.	.	.	.	.	+	.	.	.	.	.	.

+ = Coin Exists

+• = Coin is lost and known only from impressions, drawings or descriptions.

• . = Coin is not known to exist

Regnal dates		Gold						Silver (Bronze with Silver Wash)				Medallion in Bronze or Brass	Brass	Bronze	
		Multiple Aurei	Octonio	Quaternio	Binio	Aureus	Half Aureus	Medallion	Antoninianus	Denarius	Quinarius		As	Semis	Small Bronze
Early March 268-Mid-Jan. 270	**Claudius** (II), Marcus Aurelius Claudius, called Gothicus	+•	+	·	·	+	·	+	+	·	+	+	+	·	·
Mid 268	**Laelianus,** Ulpius Cornelius Laelianus, in Lyon	·	·	·	·	+	·	·	+	·	·	·	·	·	·
Mid-late 268	**Marius,** Marcus Aurelius Marius, in Cologne, later in Lyon	+•	·	·	·	+	·	·	+	·	·	·	·	·	·
Late 268-Late 270	**Victorinus,** Marcus Piavvonius Victorinus, in the West	·	·	·	·	+	+	·	+	·	+	+	·	·	·
Ca. late 270	**Domitianus,** in Lyon	·	·	·	·	·	·	·	+	·	·	·	·	·	·
Late 270 or early 271 -mid 273	**Tetricus** the elder, Caius Pius Esuvius Tetricus, in the West	+•	·	·	·	+	+	·	+	·	·	·	·	·	·
	Divus Victorinus	·	·	·	·	·	·	·	+	·	·	·	·	·	·
	Caius Pius Esuvius Tetricus the younger (son and heir apparent)	·	·	·	·	+	·	·	+	·	·	+	·	·	·
	Tetricus the elder and Tetricus the younger	+•	·	·	·	+	+•	·	·	·	·	·	·	·	·
Mid Jan. -late March 270	**Quintillus,** Marcus Aurelius Claudius Quintillus, brother of Claudius II	·	·	·	·	+	·	·	+	·	·	·	·	·	·
Early March 270-Sept. 275	**Aurelianus,** Lucius Domitius Aurelianus	·	·	+•	+	+	·	·	+	+	·	·	+	+	+
	Divus Claudius or Divus Claudius Gothicus	·	·	·	·	·	·	·	+	·	·	·	·	·	·
	Severina (consort)	·	·	·	·	·	·	·	+	+	·	·	·	·	+
	Aurelianus and Severina	·	·	·	·	·	·	·	·	·	·	·	·	+	+
	Aurelianus and Vabalathus, son of Odainath, King of Palmyra, as vir consularis rex imperator dux Romanorum	·	·	·	·	·	·	·	+	·	·	·	·	·	·
Ca. March 271-Ca. mid 272	**Vabalathus,** in the Orient	·	·	·	·	·	·	·	+	·	·	·	·	·	·
	Septimia Zenobia (mother), widow of Odainath, King of Palmyra	·	·	·	·	·	·	·	+	·	·	·	·	·	·
Ca. Oct. 275	**Interregnum** after Aurelian's death, coinage for his widow Severina with reverse inscription: concordiae militum	·	·	·	+	·	·	·	+	·	·	·	·	·	·
Oct. 275-early May 276	**Tacitus,** Marcus Claudius Tacitus	·	·	·	+	+	·	+	+	+	+	+	·	·	+
May-July 276	**Florianus,** Marcus Annius Florianus, step brother of Tacitus	·	+•	·	+	+	·	+	+	·	+	·	·	·	+
June 276-Aug. or Sept. 282	**Probus,** Marcus Aurelius Probus	·	+•	+•	+	+	+	+	+	+	+	+	·	·	+
Aug. 282-mid 283	**Carus,** Marcus Aurelius Carus	·	·	·	·	+	·	+	+	+	+	·	·	·	+
	Marcus Aurelius Carinus (son and heir apparent)	·	·	·	·	+	·	·	+	+	+	·	·	·	+
	Carus and Carinus	·	·	·	·	+	+	·	·	·	·	+	·	·	·
	Marcus Aurelius Numerianus (son and heir apparent)	·	·	·	·	+	·	·	+	·	·	·	·	·	·
	Carus, Carinus and Numerianus	·	+•	·	·	·	·	·	·	·	·	·	·	·	·

+ = Coin Exists

+• = Coin is lost and known only from impressions, drawings or descriptions.

• = Coin is not known to exist

Regnal dates		Gold					Silver		Silver (Bronze with Silver Wash)							Medallion in Bronze or Brass	Bronze
		Octonio	Quaternio	Binio	Aureus	Half Aureus	Argenteus	Half Argenteus	Medallion	Double Antoninianus	Antoninianus	Denarius	Half Antoninianus	Quinarius	Follis		Half Small Bronze
Early-mid 283	**Carus** and **Carinus**	•	+	•	•	•	•	•	•	•	+	•	•	•	•	•	•
Early 283-early summer 285	**Carinus,** Marcus Aurelius Carinus	+•	+	•	+	+•	•	•	+	•	+	+	•	+	•	•	+
	Magnia Urbica (consort)	•	•	•	+	•	•	•	•	•	+	•	•	+	•	+	+
	Carinus and Magnia Urbica	•	•	•	+	+•	•	•	•	•	•	•	•	•	•	•	•
	Divus Nigrinianus (son)	•	•	•	+	•	•	•	•	•	+	•	•	•	•	•	•
	Divus Numerianus (brother)	•	•	•	•	•	•	•	•	•	+	•	•	•	•	•	•
283-284	**Carinus** and **Numerianus**	+•	•	•	+•	+•	•	•	•	•	•	•	•	•	•	•	•
	Divus Carus (father)	•	•	•	+	•	•	•	•	•	+	•	•	•	•	•	•
Mid 283-Nov. 284	**Numerianus,** Marcus Aurelius Numerianus	+•	+	•	+	•	•	•	+	•	+	+	•	+	•	•	+
Fall 284	**Julianus,** Marcus Aurelius Julianus, in Pannonia	•	•	•	+	•	•	•	•	•	+	•	•	•	•	•	•
17 Nov. 284-1 May 305	**Diocletianus,** Caius Valerius Diocletianus	+	+	+	+	+	+	+	+	+	+	+	+	+	+	+	+
1 April 286-1 May 305	**Maximianus** (I), Marcus Aurelius Valerius Maximianus, called **Herculius**	+	+	+•	+	+	+	+	+	+	+	+	+	+	+	+	+
286-305	**Diocletianus** and **Maximianus** (I)	+	+	+	+	+•	•	•	+	•	•	•	•	•	+	•	•
Early 286-early 293	**Carausius,** Marcus Aurelius Mausaeus Carausius, in Britain	•	•	•	+	•	+	•	•	•	+	•	•	•	•	•	•
	Diocletianus	•	•	•	+	•	•	•	•	•	+	•	•	•	•	•	•
	Maximianus (I)	•	•	•	+	•	•	•	•	•	+	•	•	•	•	•	•
	Carausius, Diocletianus and Maximianus (I)	•	•	•	•	•	•	•	•	•	+	•	•	•	•	•	•
Early 293-mid 296	**Allectus** in Britain	•	•	•	+	•	•	•	•	•	+	•	•	•	•	•	•
293-305	**Diocletianus** and **Constantius** (I)	•	•	•	+	+•	•	•	•	•	•	•	•	•	+	•	•
293-305	**Diocletianus** and **Maximianus** (II)	•	•	•	•	+•	•	•	•	•	•	•	•	•	+	•	•
293-305	**Maximianus** (I) and **Constantius** (I)	•	•	•	•	+•	•	•	•	•	•	•	•	•	+	•	•
293-305	**Maximianus (I)** and **Maximianus** (II)	•	+•	•	•	+•	•	•	•	•	•	•	•	•	+	•	•
293-305	**Diocletianus, Maximianus** (I), **Constantius** (I) and **Maximianus** (II)	+	•	•	•	•	•	•	•	•	•	•	•	•	•	•	•

- + = Coin Exists
- +̣ = Coin is lost and known only from impressions, drawings or descriptions.
- • = Coin is not known to exist

Regnal dates								Gold Piece of																					Bron
		Medallion	Octonio	Quaternio	Binio	Aureus	Half Aureus	36 Scripula	18 Scripula	12 Scripula	8 Scripula	6 Scripula	4 Scripula	2 Scripula	1½ Scripula	Medallion	Argenteus	Half Argenteus	Heavy Argenteus	Light Miliarese	Medallion	Double Antoninianus	Antoninianus	Denarius	Half Antoninianus	Quinarius	Follis	Half Follis	Small Bronze
1 March 293-25 July 305	**Constantius** (I), Flavius Valerius Constantius, called **Chlorus**	·	+	+	+	+	+	·	·	·	·	·	·	·	·	·	+	+	·	·	+	+	+	+	+	+	+	·	+
1 March 293-5 May 311	**Maximianus** (II) Galeris Valerius Maximianus, called **Galerius**	·	+	+	+	+	+	·	·	·	·	·	·	·	·	·	+	+	·	·	+	+	+	+	+	+	+	·	+
	Marcus Aurelius Maximianus (I) as **Senior Augustus**	·	·	·	·	·	·	·	·	·	·	·	·	·	·	·	·	·	·	·	·	·	·	·	·	·	+	·	·
	Galeria Valeria (consort, daughter of Diocletianus)	·	·	·	·	+	·	·	·	·	·	·	·	·	·	·	·	·	·	·	·	·	·	·	·	·	+	·	·
	Galerius Valerius Maximinus (nephew and adopted son)	·	·	·	+	+	·	·	·	·	·	·	·	·	·	·	·	·	·	·	·	·	·	·	·	·	+	·	·
	Flavius Valerius Constantinus	·	·	·	·	+	·	·	·	·	·	·	·	·	·	·	·	·	·	·	·	·	·	·	·	·	+	·	·
	Valerius Licinianus Licinius	·	·	·	·	+	·	·	·	·	·	·	·	·	·	·	·	·	·	·	·	·	·	·	·	·	+	·	·
Aug. 296-March 297	**Domitianus**, Lucius Domitius Domitianus, in Egypt	·	·	·	·	+	·	·	·	·	·	·	·	·	·	·	·	·	·	·	·	·	·	·	·	·	+	·	·
1 May 305-early 307	**Severus** (II), Flavius Valerius Severus	·	·	·	+	+	·	·	·	·	·	·	·	·	·	·	+	·	·	·	·	·	+	+	·	+	+	·	·
305-307	**Severus** (II), and **Maximinus** (II)	·	·	·	·	·	·	·	·	·	·	·	·	·	·	·	·	·	·	·	·	·	·	·	·	·	+	·	·
1 May 305-summer 313	**Maximinus** (II), Galerius Valerius Maximinus,	·	·	·	·	+	·	·	·	·	·	·	·	·	·	·	+	·	·	·	·	·	+	+	+	+	+	·	·
	called **Daia**, as Senior Augustus	·	·	·	·	·	·	·	·	·	·	·	·	·	·	·	·	·	·	·	·	·	·	·	·	·	+	·	·
	Marcus Aurelius Valerius Maximianus (I), as Senior Augustus	·	·	·	·	·	·	·	·	·	·	·	·	·	·	·	·	·	·	·	·	·	·	·	·	·	+	·	·
	Galerius Valerius Maximianus (II), (uncle and adopted father)	·	·	·	+	+	·	·	·	·	·	·	·	·	·	·	·	·	·	·	·	·	·	·	·	·	+	·	·
	Galeria Valeria (consort of Maximianus II)	·	·	·	+	+	·	·	·	·	·	·	·	·	·	·	·	·	·	·	·	·	·	·	·	·	+	·	·
	Flavius Valerius Constantinus	·	·	·	·	+	·	·	·	·	·	·	·	·	·	·	·	·	·	·	·	·	·	·	·	·	+	·	·
	Valerius Licinianus Licinius (often spelled Licinnius)	·	·	·	·	+	·	·	·	·	·	·	·	·	·	·	·	·	·	·	·	·	·	·	·	·	+	·	·
	Memorial issues in the name of Maximinus for:																												
	Divus Maximianus (II), (uncle and adopted father)	·	·	·	·	·	·	·	·	·	·	·	·	·	·	·	·	·	·	·	·	·	·	·	·	·	+	·	·
	City issues without the name of Maximinus for:																												
	Alexandria	·	·	·	·	·	·	·	·	·	·	·	·	·	·	·	·	·	·	·	·	·	·	·	+	+	·	·	·
	Antioch	·	·	·	·	·	·	·	·	·	·	·	·	·	·	·	·	·	·	·	·	·	·	·	+	·	·	·	·
	Nicomedia	·	·	·	·	·	·	·	·	·	·	·	·	·	·	·	·	·	·	·	·	·	·	·	·	+	·	·	·
305-307	**Emperors of the 2nd and 3rd Tetrarchies,** Constantius (I), Maximianus (II), Severus (II), Maximinus (II) and Constantinus for the retired emperors:																												
	Diocletanus as Senior Augustus	·	·	·	·	+	·	·	·	·	·	·	·	·	·	·	·	·	·	·	·	·	+	·	·	·	+	·	·
	Maximianus (I) as Senior Augustus	·	·	·	·	+	·	·	·	·	·	·	·	·	·	·	·	·	·	·	·	·	+	·	·	·	+	·	·
26 July 306-22 may 337	**Constantinus**, Flavius Valerius Constantinus, the Great	+	·	·	·	+	·	+	+	+	+	+	+	+	+	+	+	+	+	+	+	·	+	+	+	+	+	+	·
	Diocletianus, as Senior Augustus	·	·	·	·	·	·	·	·	·	·	·	·	·	·	·	·	·	·	·	·	·	·	·	·	+	+	·	·
	Marcus Aurelius Valerius Maximianus (I) (father-in-law) as Senior Augustus	·	·	·	·	·	·	·	·	·	·	·	·	·	·	·	+	+	·	·	·	·	·	·	·	+	+	·	·
	Divus Constantius (I) (father)	·	·	·	·	·	·	·	·	·	·	·	+	·	·	·	·	·	·	·	·	·	·	+	·	·	+	·	·
	Maximianus (II)	·	·	·	·	·	·	·	·	·	·	·	+	·	·	·	+	+	·	·	·	·	·	·	·	·	+	·	·
	Galerius Valerius Maximinus (II)	·	·	·	·	·	·	·	·	·	·	·	+	·	·	·	+	+	·	·	·	·	·	·	·	·	+	·	·
	Marcus Aurelius Valerius Maxentius (brother-in-law)	·	·	·	·	·	·	·	·	·	·	·	+	·	·	·	·	·	·	·	·	·	·	·	·	·	+	·	·

+ = Coin Exists

+• = Coin is lost and known only from impressions, drawings or descriptions.

. = Coin is not known to exist

Regnal dates		Gold											Silver				Silver (Bronze with Silver Wash)					
				Gold Piece of																		
		Medallion	Aureus	More than 36 Scrip.	36 Scripula	18 Scripula	12 Scripula	8 Scripula	6 Scripula	4 Scripula	2 Scripula	1½ Scripula	Argenteus	Half Argenteus	Heavy Argenteus	More than 36 Scripula	Medallion	Antoninianus	Denarius	Half Antoninianus	Quinarius	Follis
	(Constantine continued)																					
	Licinius the elder (brother-in-law)	.	+	.	.	.	.	.	.	+	.	+	+	.	+	.	+	.	.	+	+	+
	Valerius Licinianus Licinius the younger (son of Licinius and heir apparent)	.	.	.	.	+	.	+	.	+	.	.	.	.	+	.	+	.	.	.	.	+
	Flavia Helena (mother)	.	.	.	.	.	.	+	.	+	.	.	.	.	.	.	+	.	.	.	.	+
	Flavia Maxima Fausta (consort, daughter of Maximianus I)	.	.	.	.	.	.	+	.	+	.	.	.	+	.	.	+	.	.	.	.	+
	Constantia (sister, widow of Licinius)	.	.	.	.	.	.	.	.	.	.	.	.	.	.	.	.	.	.	.	.	+
	Flavius Julius Crispus (son and heir apparent)	+	+	.	.	.	.	+	+	+	.	+	.	.	+	.	+	.	.	.	+	+
	Flavius Claudius Constantinus the younger, (son and heir apparent)	+	+	.	+	+	+	+	+	+	+	+	+	.	+	+	+	.	.	.	+	+
	Flavius Valerius Julius Constantius (son and heir apparent)	+	+	+	+	+	+	+	+	+	+	+	+	.	.	+	+	.	.	.	.	+
	Flavius Delmatius (nephew and heir apparent)	.	.	.	.	.	.	.	.	+	.	.	+	.	.	.	.	.	.	.	.	+
	Constantinus, Crispus and Constantinus the younger	.	.	.	.	+	.	+	+	.	.	.	.	.	.	+	.	.	.	.	.	.
	Constantinus, Crispus and Constantius	.	.	.	.	.	.	+	+•	.	.	.	.	.	.	.	.	.	.	.	.	.
	Constantinus, Constantinus the younger and Constantius	.	.	.	.	.	.	+•	+	.	.	.	.	.	.	.	.	.	.	.	.	.
	Crispus and Constantinus the younger	.	.	.	.	.	.	.	+	.	.	.	.	.	.	.	.	.	.	.	.	.
	Flavius Hannibalianus (nephew), intended Persian Shah	.	.	.	.	.	.	.	.	.	.	.	+	.	.	.	.	.	.	.	.	+
	City issues for:																					
	Urbs Roma	.	.	.	.	.	.	.	.	.	.	.	.	.	.	.	+	.	.	.	.	+
	Constantinopolis	.	.	.	.	.	.	.	.	.	.	.	.	.	.	.	+	.	.	.	.	+
	Populus Romanus	.	.	.	.	.	.	.	.	.	.	.	.	.	.	.	.	.	.	.	+	.
	Memorial issues for:																					
	Divus Claudius (II), (assumed ancestor)	.	.	.	.	.	.	.	.	.	.	.	.	.	.	.	.	.	.	+	+	+
	Divus Maximianus (I), (father-in-law)	.	.	.	.	.	.	.	.	.	.	.	.	.	.	.	.	.	.	+	+	+
	Divus Constantius (I), (father)	.	.	.	.	.	.	.	.	.	.	.	.	.	.	.	.	.	.	+	+	+
28 Oct. 306-28 Oct. 312	**Maxentius,** Marcus Aurelius Valerius Maxentius, in Italy and Africa	.	+	.	.	.	.	.	.	.	.	.	+	+•	.	.	+	+	+	.	.	+
	Maximianus (I) as Senior Augustus or as Divus Augustus (father)	.	+	.	.	.	.	.	.	.	.	.	+	.	.	.	.	.	.	.	.	+
	Divus Maximianus (II) (father-in-law)	.	.	.	.	.	.	.	.	.	.	.	.	.	.	.	.	.	.	.	.	+
	Divus Constantius (I) (brother-in-law)	.	.	.	.	.	.	.	.	.	.	.	.	.	.	.	.	.	.	.	.	+
	Galerius Valerius Maximinus	.	+	.	.	.	.	.	.	.	.	.	.	.	.	.	.	.	.	.	.	+
	Flavius Valerius Constantinus (brother-in-law)	.	+	.	.	.	.	.	.	.	.	.	+	.	.	.	.	.	.	.	.	+
	Divus Romulus (son)	.	.	.	.	.	.	.	.	.	.	.	.	.	.	.	.	.	+	.	.	+
	Memorial issues in the name of Maxentius for:																					
	Divus Maximianus (I) (father)	.	.	.	.	.	.	.	.	.	.	.	.	.	.	.	.	.	.	.	.	+
	Divus Maximianus (II) (father-in-law)	.	.	.	.	.	.	.	.	.	.	.	.	.	.	.	.	.	.	.	.	+
	Divus Constantius (I) (brother-in-law)	.	.	.	.	.	.	.	.	.	.	.	.	.	.	.	.	.	.	.	.	+
	Divus Romulus (son)	.	.	.	.	.	.	.	.	.	.	.	.	.	.	.	.	.	.	.	.	+
11 Nov. 308-Sept. 324	**Licinius** the elder, Valerius Licinianus Licinius	.	+	.	.	.	.	.	.	.	.	.	.	.	.	.	.	+	.	.	.	+
	Galerius Valerius Maximianus (II)	.	+	.	.	.	.	.	.	.	.	.	.	.	.	.	.	.	.	.	.	+
	Galeria Valeria, (consort of Maximianus (II)	.	+	.	.	.	.	.	.	.	.	.	.	.	.	.	.	.	.	.	.	+
	Galerius Valerius Maximinus (II)	.	+	.	.	.	.	.	.	.	.	.	.	.	.	.	.	.	.	.	.	+
	Flavius Valerius Constantinus (brother-in-law)	.	+	.	.	.	.	.	.	.	.	.	.	.	.	.	.	+	.	.	.	+

+ = Coin Exists

+• = Coin is lost and known only from impressions, drawings or descriptions.

• = Coin is not known to exist

Regnal dates		Gold			Gold Piece of								Silver						Silver (Bronze with Silver Wash)					
		Medallion	Octonio	Aureus	36 Scripula	18 Scripula	12 Scripula	8 Scripula	6 Scripula	4 Scripula Solidus	2 Scripula Semissis	1½ Scripula	Stamped Silver Bars	Quadruple Argenteus	Argenteus	Light Miliarese	Siliqua	Heavy Miliarese	Medallion	Antoninianus	Follis	1½ Maiorina	Maiorina	Centenionalis
	Licinius the Elder (continued)																							
	Valerius Licinianus Constantinus Licinius the younger (son and heir apparent)	•	•	+	•	•	•	•	•	•	•	•	•	•	•	•	•	•	•	+	+	•	•	•
	Licinius the elder and Licinius the younger	•	+	•	•	•	•	•	•	•	•	•	•	•	•	•	•	•	•	•	+	•	•	•
	Flavius Julius Crispus (son of Constantinus and heir-apparent)	•	•	+	•	•	•	•	•	•	•	•	•	•	•	•	•	•	•	+	+	•	•	•
	Flavius Claudius Constantinus the younger (son of Constantinus and heir apparent)	•	•	+	•	•	•	•	•	•	•	•	•	•	•	•	•	•	•	+	+	•	•	•
	Licinius the elder and Constantinus	•	•	•	•	•	•	•	•	•	•	•	•	•	•	•	•	•	•	•	+	•	•	•
	Licinius the younger and Constantinus the younger	•	•	•	•	•	•	•	•	•	•	•	•	•	•	•	•	•	•	•	+	•	•	•
June 308-June 311	**Alexander**, in Africa	•	•	+	•	•	•	•	•	•	•	•	•	•	•	•	•	•	•	•	+	•	•	•
Ca. Oct.-Nov. 314	**Valens**, Aurelius Valerius Valens, co-regent with Licinius	•	•	•	•	•	•	•	•	•	•	•	•	•	•	•	•	•	•	•	+	•	•	•
Ca. July-Sept. 324	**Martinianus**, Marcus Martinianus, co-regent with Licinius	•	•	•	•	•	•	•	•	•	•	•	•	•	•	•	•	•	•	+	•	•	•	•
337-340	**Constantinus** (II), **Constans** and **Constantius** (II) for:																							
	Divus Constantinus (father)	•	•	•	•	•	•	•	•	•	•	•	•	•	•	•	•	•	•	•	+	•	•	•
	Flavia Maxima Theodora (wife of their grandfather, Constantius I)	•	•	•	•	•	•	•	•	•	•	•	•	•	•	•	•	•	•	•	+	•	•	•
	Flavia Julia Helena (grandmother)	•	•	•	•	•	•	•	•	•	•	•	•	•	•	•	•	•	•	•	+	•	•	•
	City issues for:																							
	Urbs Roma	•	•	•	•	•	•	•	•	•	•	•	•	•	•	•	•	•	+	•	+	•	•	•
	Constantinopolis	•	•	•	•	•	•	•	•	•	•	•	•	•	•	•	•	•	+	•	+	•	•	•
9 Sept. 337-Spring 340	**Constantinus** (II) Flavius Claudius Julius Victor Constantinus	+	•	•	•	•	•	+	+	+	•	+	•	•	+	+	•	+	+	•	+	•	•	•
9 Sept. 337-Early 350	**Constans** Flavius Julius Constans	+	•	+	+	+	+	+	+	+	+	+	•	+	+	+	•	+	+	•	+	•	+	+
340-350	**Constantius** (II) and **Constans**	•	•	•	+	•	•	•	•	•	•	•	•	•	•	•	•	•	•	•	•	•	•	•
9 Sept. 337-3 Nov. 361	**Constantius** (II), Flavius Julius Constantius	+	•	+	+	+	+	+	+	+	+	+	•	+	+	+	+	+	+	•	+	+	+	+
	Flavius Claudius Constantius, called Gallus (cousin and heir-apparent)	•	•	•	•	•	•	•	•	+	+	+	•	+	+	+	•	+	+	•	•	•	+	+
	Flavius Claudius Julianus (cousin and heir-apparent)	•	•	•	•	•	•	+	•	+	•	+	•	•	+	•	+	•	+	•	•	•	•	+
	City issues for:																							
	Urbs Roma	•	•	•	•	•	•	•	•	•	•	•	•	•	•	•	•	•	+	•	•	•	•	•
18 Jan. 350-10 Aug. 350	**Magnentius**, Flavius Magnus Magnentius, in the West	•	•	+	•	+•	•	+	+	+	+	•	+	+	+	+	•	+	+	•	•	+	+	+
	Magnus Decentius (brother and heir-apparent)	•	•	•	•	•	•	•	+	+	+	•	•	•	+	+	•	+	+	•	•	+	+	+
	Constantius (II)	•	•	•	•	•	•	•	•	•	•	•	•	•	•	•	•	•	•	•	•	•	+	•
1 March-25 Dec. 350	**Vetranio**, in Illyricum	•	•	•	•	•	•	•	•	+	•	•	•	•	+	+	•	•	•	•	•	•	+	+
	Constantius (II)	•	•	•	•	•	•	•	•	•	•	•	•	•	•	•	•	•	•	•	•	•	+	+
3-30 June 350	**Nepotianus**, in Rome, Flavius Popilius Nepotianus Constantinus, nephew of Constantine the Great	•	•	•	•	•	•	•	•	+	•	•	•	•	•	•	•	•	•	•	•	•	+	•
	Constantius (II) (cousin)	•	•	•	•	•	•	•	•	•	•	•	•	•	•	•	•	•	•	•	•	•	+	•

+ = Coin Exists

+• = Coin is lost and known only from impressions, drawings or descriptions.

• = Coin is not known to exist

Regnal dates		Gold										Silver						Silver (Bronze with Silver Wash)							Medallion in Bronze or Brass
		Aureus	Gold Piece of: More than 36 Scrip.	36 Scripula	18 Scripula	12 Scripula	8 Scripula	6 Scripula	4 Scripula	2 Scripula	1½ Scripula	Quadruple Argenteus	Argenteus	Light Miliarese	Siliqua	Half Siliqua	Heavy Miliarese	Medallion	Medallion	Small Bronze	Double Maiorina	Maiorina	Centenionalis	Quarter Maiorina	
11 Aug.- 7 Sept. 355	**Maximianus** (III), in Cologne, same as Silvanus	•	•	•	•	•	•	•	•	•	•	•	+	•	•	•	•	•	•	•	•	•	•	•	•
Feb. 360- 26 June 363	**Julianus,** Flavius Claudius Julianus, called **Apostata**	•	•	•	•	•	•	•	+	•	+	•	•	+	+	•	•	+	+	+	•	•	+	•	•
	Constantius (II) (cousin and brother-in-law)	•	•	•	•	•	•	•	+	•	•	•	•	+	+	•	•	•	•	•	•	•	•	•	•
27 June 363- 17 Feb. 364	**Jovianus**	•	•	+•	•	•	•	•	+	•	•	•	•	+	+	•	•	+	+	+	•	•	•	•	•
26 Feb. 364- 17 Nov. 375	**Valentinianus** (I)	•	•	+	+	+	+	+	+	+	+	+	+	+	+	•	+	+	+	+	•	+	+	•	•
28 March 364- 9 Aug. 378	**Valens,** brother of Valentinianus (I)	•	+	+	+	•	+	+	+	+	+	+	+	+	+	•	+	+	+	•	•	+	+	•	•
28 Sept. 365- 27 May 366	**Procopius,** in Thrace and Asia Minor, relative of Julianus	•	•	•	•	•	•	•	+	•	•	•	•	•	+	•	•	•	•	+	+	+	+	•	•
24 Aug. 367- 25 Aug. 383	**Gratianus,** son of Valentinianus (I)	+	•	+•	+	•	+	•	+	+	+	•	+	+	+	+	+	+	•	•	•	+	+	+	•
284-375	**Heathen issues,** originating in the Rome mint under the influence of the Isis Cult:																								
	Deus Serapis or Deus Sarapis	•	•	•	•	•	•	•	•	•	•	•	•	•	•	•	•	•	•	•	•	•	•	•	+
	Isis Faria	•	•	•	•	•	•	•	•	•	•	•	•	•	•	•	•	•	•	•	•	•	•	•	+
	Serapis and Isis	•	•	•	•	•	•	•	•	•	•	•	•	•	•	•	•	•	•	•	•	•	•	•	+
	Diocletianus	•	•	•	•	•	•	•	•	•	•	•	•	•	•	•	•	•	•	•	•	•	•	•	+
	Maximianus (I)	•	•	•	•	•	•	•	•	•	•	•	•	•	•	•	•	•	•	•	•	•	•	•	+
	Constantius (I)	•	•	•	•	•	•	•	•	•	•	•	•	•	•	•	•	•	•	•	•	•	•	•	+
	Maximianus (II)	•	•	•	•	•	•	•	•	•	•	•	•	•	•	•	•	•	•	•	•	•	•	•	+
	Constantinus the Great	•	•	•	•	•	•	•	•	•	•	•	•	•	•	•	•	•	•	•	•	•	•	•	+
	Licinius the elder	•	•	•	•	•	•	•	•	•	•	•	•	•	•	•	•	•	•	•	•	•	•	•	+
	Crispus	•	•	•	•	•	•	•	•	•	•	•	•	•	•	•	•	•	•	•	•	•	•	•	+
	Constantinus (II)	•	•	•	•	•	•	•	•	•	•	•	•	•	•	•	•	•	•	•	•	•	•	•	+
	Constans	•	•	•	•	•	•	•	•	•	•	•	•	•	•	•	•	•	•	•	•	•	•	•	+
	Constantius (II)	•	•	•	•	•	•	•	•	•	•	•	•	•	•	•	•	•	•	•	•	•	•	•	+
	Magnentius	•	•	•	•	•	•	•	•	•	•	•	•	•	•	•	•	•	•	•	•	•	•	•	+
	Constantius Gallus	•	•	•	•	•	•	•	•	•	•	•	•	•	•	•	•	•	•	•	•	•	•	•	+
	Julianus	•	•	•	•	•	•	•	•	•	•	•	•	•	•	•	•	•	•	•	•	•	•	•	+
	Jovianus	•	•	•	•	•	•	•	•	•	•	•	•	•	•	•	•	•	•	•	•	•	•	•	+
	Valentinianus (I)	•	•	•	•	•	•	•	•	•	•	•	•	•	•	•	•	•	•	•	•	•	•	•	+
	Valens	•	•	•	•	•	•	•	•	•	•	•	•	•	•	•	•	•	•	•	•	•	•	•	+
	Gratianus	•	•	•	•	•	•	•	•	•	•	•	•	•	•	•	•	•	•	•	•	•	•	•	+
	Roma	•	•	•	•	•	•	•	•	•	•	•	•	•	•	•	•	•	•	•	•	•	•	•	+
	Constantinopolis																								

+ = Coin Exists

+• = Coin is lost and known only from impressions, drawings or descriptions.

• = Coin is not known to exist

Regnal dates		Gold											Silver								Silver (Bronze w. Silver Wash)			
				Gold Piece of																				
		Aureus	Stamped Gold Bars	36 Scripula	18 Scripula	12 Scripula	8 Scripula	6 Scripula	4 Scripula Solidus	2 Scripula Semissis	1½ Scripula	Tremissis	Silver Stamped Bars	Quadruple Argenteus	Argenteus	Light Miliarese	Siliqua	Half Siliqua	15 X Heavy Miliarese	Heavy Miliarese	Medallion	Maiorina	Centenionalis	Quarter Maiorina
22 Nov. 375-15 May 392	**Valentinianus** (II), son of Valentinianus (I)	+	•	+	•	•	+	•	+	+	+	+	•	+	+	+	+	+	•	+	+	+	+	+
19 Jan. 379-17 Jan. 395	**Theodosius** (I), the Great	•	•	+	•	•	•	•	+	+	+	+	•	+	•	+	+	+	•	+	+	+	+	+
	Aelia Flaccilla (consort)	•	•	•	•	•	•	•	+	•	•	•	•	•	•	•	+	•	•	•	•	+	•	+
	Maximus (brother-in-law)	•	•	•	•	•	•	•	+	•	•	•	•	•	•	•	•	•	•	•	•	+	•	•
19 Jan.-24 Feb. 379	**Gratianus, Valentinianus** (II) and **Theodosius** (I)	•	+	•	•	•	•	•	•	•	•	•	+	•	•	•	•	•	•	•	•	•	•	•
19 Jan. 383-1 May 408	**Arcadius**, son of Theodosius (I)	+	•	+•	+	+	•	+	+	+	+	+	•	+	•	+	+	+	•	+	•	+	+	+
	Aelia Eudoxia (consort)	•	•	•	•	•	•	•	+	+	•	+	•	•	•	•	+	+	•	•	•	•	+	•
Spring 383-28 Aug. 388	**Magnus Maximus**, in the West	•	•	•	•	•	•	•	+	+	•	+	•	•	•	+	+	•	•	+	•	+	•	+
	Theodosius, (brother-in-law)	•	•	•	•	•	•	•	+	•	•	•	•	•	•	•	•	•	•	•	•	•	•	•
Ca. 387-late 388	**Flavius Victor**, son of Magnus Maximus	•	•	•	•	•	•	•	+	+	•	+	•	•	•	•	+	•	•	•	•	•	•	+
22 Aug. 392-6 Sept. 394	**Eugenius**, in the West	•	•	•	•	•	+	•	+	•	•	+	•	•	•	+	+	+	•	+	•	•	•	+
	Theodosius (I)	•	•	•	•	•	•	•	+	•	•	•	•	•	•	•	+	•	•	•	•	•	•	+
	Arcadius	•	•	•	•	•	•	•	+	•	•	•	•	•	•	•	+	•	•	•	•	•	•	+
	Honorius	•	•	•	•	•	•	•	•	•	•	•	•	•	•	•	•	•	•	•	•	•	•	+
23 Jan. 393-15 Aug. 423	**Honorius**, son of Theodosius (I)	•	•	+•	+	•	•	+	+	+	•	+	•	+	•	+	+	+	•	+	•	+	+	+
10 Jan. 402-28 July 450	**Theodosius** (II), son of Arcadius	•	•	•	•	•	•	•	+	+	•	+	•	•	•	+	+	+	•	•	•	•	+	+
	Aelia Pulcheria (sister)	•	•	•	•	•	•	•	+	+	•	+	•	•	•	•	+	•	•	•	•	•	+	•
	Aelia Eudocia (consort)	•	•	•	•	•	•	•	+	+	•	+	•	•	•	•	+	•	•	•	•	•	+	•
Mid 407-Summer 411	**Constantinus** (III), in the West	•	•	•	•	•	•	•	+	•	•	+	•	•	•	•	+	•	•	•	•	•	•	•
Nov. 409-June 410	**Priscus Attalus**, in Rome	•	•	•	•	•	•	•	+	•	•	+	•	•	•	•	•	•	+	•	•	•	+	•
409-411	**Maximus**, in Spain	•	•	•	•	•	•	•	•	•	•	•	•	•	•	•	+	•	•	•	•	•	•	•
410-early 411	**Constans**, son of Constantinus III	•	•	•	•	•	•	•	•	•	•	•	•	•	•	•	+	•	•	•	•	•	•	•
Summer 411-early 413	**Jovinus**, in Gaul	•	•	•	•	•	•	•	+	•	•	•	•	•	•	•	+	•	•	•	•	•	•	•
412-early 413	**Sebastianus**, brother of Jovinus	•	•	•	•	•	•	•	•	•	•	•	•	•	•	•	+	•	•	•	•	•	•	•
Early 414-early 416	**Priscus Attalus**, second reign, in Gaul	•	•	•	•	•	•	•	+	•	•	•	•	•	•	+	+	•	•	•	•	•	•	•
8 Feb.-2 Sept. 421	**Constantius** (III) called Patricius	•	•	•	•	•	•	•	+	•	•	+	•	•	•	•	•	•	•	•	•	•	•	•

\+ = Coin Exists

+• = Coin is lost and known only from impressions, drawings or descriptions.

• = Coin is not known to exist

Regnal dates		Gold: Gold Piece of 6 Scripula	Gold: Gold Piece of 4 Scripula Solidus	Gold: Gold Piece of 2 Scripula Semissis	Gold: Tremissis	Silver: Quadruple Argenteus	Silver: Light Miliarese	Silver: Siliqua	Silver: Half Siliqua	Silver (Bronze with Silver Wash): Maiorina	Silver (Bronze with Silver Wash): Centenionalis	Silver (Bronze with Silver Wash): Quarter Maiorina
Dec. 423- June 425	**Johannes**	•	+	•	+	•	•	+	+	•	•	+
23 Oct. 424- 16 March 455	**Valentinianus** (III), Placidius Valentinianus, son of Constantius (III)	•	+	+	+	•	•	+	+	•	•	+
	Galla Placidia (mother)	+	+	+	+	•	•	+	+	•	•	+
	Justa Grata Honoria (sister)	•	+	+	+	•	•	•	•	•	•	•
	Licinia Eudoxia (consort, daughter of Theodosius II)	•	+	•	•	•	•	•	•	•	•	•
25 Aug. 450- 26 Jan. 457	**Marcianus**	•	+	+	+	•	+	+	•	•	•	+
17 March- 31 May 455	**Petronius Maximus**	•	+	•	•	•	•	•	•	•	•	•
9 July 455- 17 Oct. 456	**Avitus**, Maecilius Avitus	•	+	•	+	•	•	+	•	•	•	+
7 Feb. 457- 18 Jan. 474	**Leo** (I), the Great	•	+	+	+	+	+•	+	+	+	+	+
	Aelia Verina (consort)	•	+	•	+	•	•	•	•	+	•	•
1 April 457- 7 Aug. 461	**Maiorianus**, Julius Maiorianus	•	+	•	+	•	•	•	+	•	+	•
19 Nov. 461- 14 Nov. 465	**Libius Severus**	•	+	+	+	•	•	+	+	•	•	+
12 April 467- 11 July 472	**Anthemius**, Procopius Anthemius	•	+	+	+	•	•	•	+	•	•	+
	Aelia Marcia Eufemia (consort, daughter of Marcianus)	•	+	•	•	•	•	•	•	•	•	•
April- 2 Nov. 472	**Anicius Olybrius**	•	+	•	+	•	•	•	•	•	•	•
3 March 473- Spring 474	**Glycerius**	•	+	•	+	•	•	•	+	•	•	+
9 Feb.- early fall 474	**Leo** (II) and his father **Zeno**	•	+	+	+	•	•	•	•	•	•	•
early fall 474- 9 April 491	**Zeno**	•	+	+	+	•	+	+	+	•	+	+
	Zeno and his son Leo (II) as heir apparent	•	+	•	+	•	•	•	•	•	•	•
	Aelia Ariadne (consort, daughter of Leo I)	•	+	•	+	•	•	•	•	•	•	•
19 or 24 June 474 - 28 Aug. 475	**Julius Nepos**	•	+	•	+	•	•	+	+	•	•	+
9 Jan. 475- late Aug. 476	**Basiliscus**, (brother-in-law of Leo (I)	•	+	•	+	•	+•	+•	+•	•	•	+
	Basiliscus and Marcus, son and heir-apparent	•	+	•	+	•	•	•	•	•	•	•
	Aelia Zenonis (consort)	•	+	•	•	•	•	•	•	•	•	•
31 Oct. 475- Sept. 476	**Romulus Augustus**	•	+	•	+	•	•	•	+	•	•	+
11 April 491-	**Anastasius**	•	+	+	+	•	•	+	•	•	•	+